STATISTICS

5

Walker Maths Essentials: Statistics 5
1st Edition
Charlotte Walker
Victoria Walker

Cover and text design: Cheryl Smith, Macarn Design
Production controller: Siew Han Ong

Any URLs contained in this publication were checked for currency during the production process. Note, however, that the publisher cannot vouch for the ongoing currency of URLs.

Acknowledgements
Cover photo courtesy of Shutterstock

The authors wish to thank past and present colleagues who have generously shared their expertise and ideas.

For product information and technology assistance,
in Australia call **1300 790 853**;
in New Zealand call **0800 449 725**

For permission to use material from this text or product, please email
aust.permissions@cengage.com

National Library of New Zealand Cataloguing-in-Publication Data
A catalogue record for this book is available from the National Library of New Zealand

978 01 7044729 4

Cengage Learning Australia
Level 5, 80 Dorcas Street
Southbank VIC 3006 Australia

Cengage Learning New Zealand
For learning solutions, visit **cengage.co.nz**

Printed in China by 1010 Printing International Limited.
1 2 3 4 5 6 7 27 26 25 24 23

CONTENTS

Glossary

Make your own glossary of key terms:

Term	Definition	Picture/Example
Theoretical probability		
Experimental probability		
Sample space		
Outcome		
Census		
Sample		
Population		
Descriptive variable		
Discrete variable		
Continuous variable		
Proportion		
Axis (plural: axes)		
Frequency		

ISBN: 9780170447294

Term	Definition	Picture/Example
Mean		
Median		
Mode		
Range		
Interquartile range		
Unusual points		
Cluster		
Bias		
Expected number		

The statistical inquiry cycle

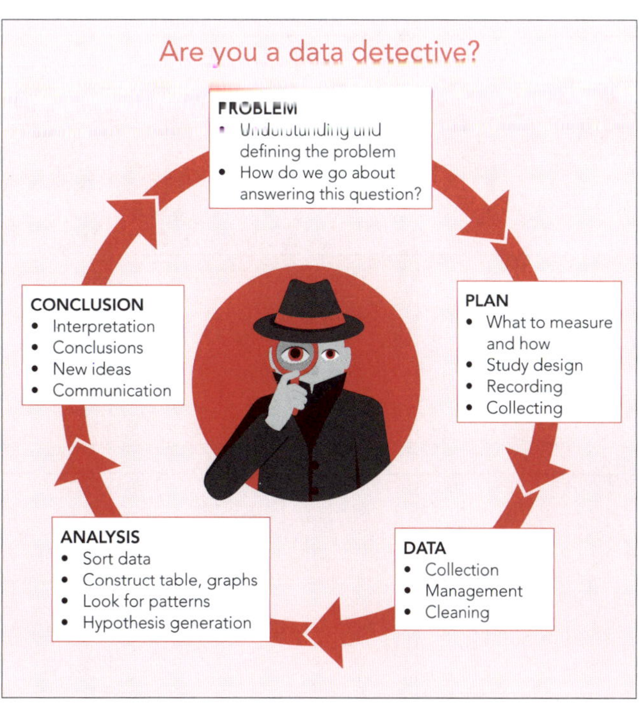

Probability

Fraction, decimal and percentage revision

Complete the table. Parts have been done for you.

Shaded circle picture	Fraction	Decimal	Percentage
	$\frac{18}{24} = \frac{}{4}$		
		$0.\dot{3}$	
			37.5%
	$\frac{26}{39} = \frac{}{3}$		
		0.875	

ISBN: 9780170447294

The probability scale

- A probability value tells us **how likely** it is that an event will occur.
- We use numbers between **0** and **1** to describe probability.

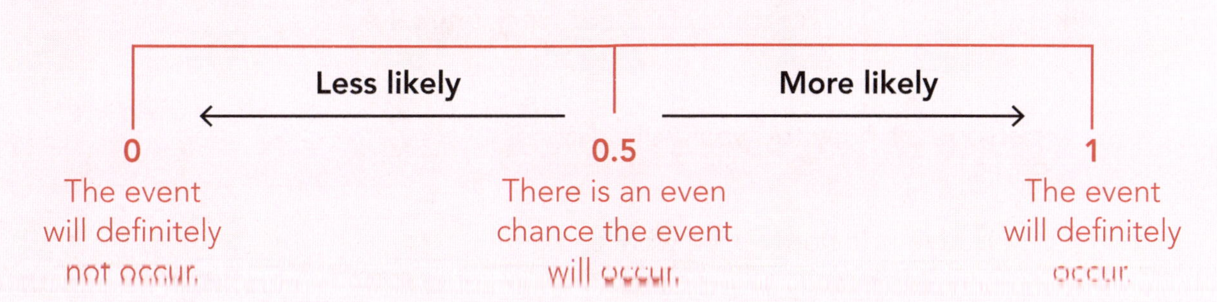

1 Write terms that match each of the probabilities on the scale below. Two have been done for you.

1 ____________________

0.9 very likely

0.7 ____________________

0.5 ____________________

0.3 ____________________

0.1 ____________________

0 impossible

2 Use each of these terms once only to describe the probability of each of these events occurring.

impossible	fifty-fifty chance	very likely	unlikely
likely	certain	very unlikely	

a A person's birthday this year will be on a Friday. ______________

b Somebody's ride home from work today is a plane. ______________

c A person was born in an odd year. ______________

d Somebody will get a live moa for their birthday. ______________

e There won't be lightning tomorrow. ______________

f A person's birthday this year will be on a weekday. ______________

g This school term will end. ______________

3 Write down an event which you think has each of the following probabilities, and discuss your answers with your neighbour or your teacher.

a **impossible** ______________

b **very unlikely** ______________

c **unlikely** ______________

d **fifty-fifty** ______________

e **likely** ______________

f **very likely** ______________

g **certain** ______________

ISBN: 9780170447294

Using numbers to describe probabilities

- Probabilities can be written as **fractions, decimals, percentages** or **proportions**.
- Sometimes, probabilities are written as '**one in** …', e.g. one in ten means $\frac{1}{10}$.
- Occasionally reasonably even probabilities are written as a ratio out of 100, e.g. 60:40 means $\frac{60}{100}$ compared with $\frac{40}{100}$.
- If you want to **compare** probabilities, it is usually easiest to convert them to **decimals**.
- You need to be able to convert probabilities to decimals using your calculator.

Examples. Convert these probabilities into decimals and state which is more likely.

1 $\frac{4}{9} = 0.4\dot{4}$ 40% = 0.4

More likely: $\frac{4}{9}$

$0.4\dot{4}$ is bigger than 0.4, so $\frac{4}{9}$ is more likely.

2 1 in 9 = $\frac{1}{9} = 0.\dot{1}$ 10% = 0.1

More likely: 1 in 9

3 $\frac{3}{7} = 0.429$ 43% = 0.43

More likely: 43%

4 3 in 8 = 0.375 $\frac{6}{15} = 0.4$

More likely: $\frac{6}{15}$

Convert these probabilities into decimals (4 dp) and state which is most likely.

1 35% = ________ 1 in 3 = ________

More likely: ____________

2 $\frac{5}{6}$ = ________ 80:20 = ________

More likely: ____________

3 65% = ________ $\frac{5}{8}$ = ________

More likely: ____________

4 $\frac{2}{7}$ = ________ 1 in 5 = ________

More likely: ____________

5 In New Zealand, the probability that a normal pregnancy results in identical twins is 0.0075. The probability that one results in triplets is 1 in 8100. Which is more likely?

____

____

6 The probability of tossing a coin 10 times and getting ten heads is 0.00098 (2 sf). The probability of throwing a die four times and getting four 6s is 1 in 1296. Which event is more likely?

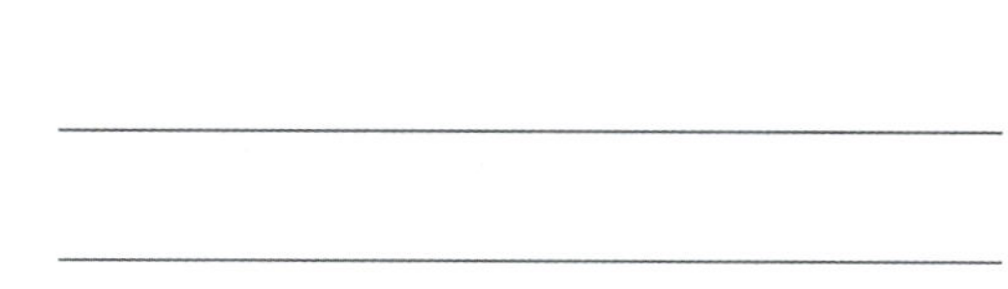

7 The probability of winning Powerball in New Zealand is one in thirty-eight million.

Write this number as a decimal to 2 sf. ____________

ISBN: 9780170447294

Sample space

- The **sample space** is a **list of the outcomes that can occur** when we do a probability experiment.

When one event occurs, make a list.

For example:

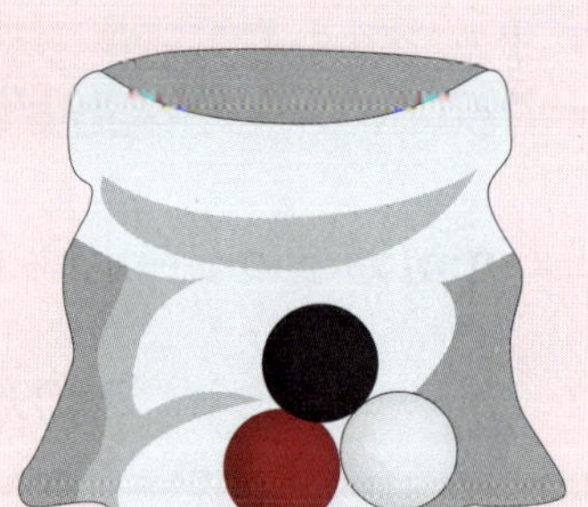

1 If you toss a coin, there are only two outcomes: head, tail.
∴ Sample space contains two items: head, tail.

2 If you pull a marble out of this bag, there are only three outcomes: red, black and white.

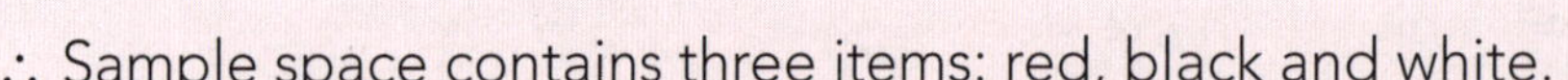

∴ Sample space contains three items: red, black and white.

When two events occur, draw a probability tree or make a table.

For example: Toss a coin and then pull a marble from the bag.

Draw a probability tree.

Use the tree to **list the outcomes** in the sample space:

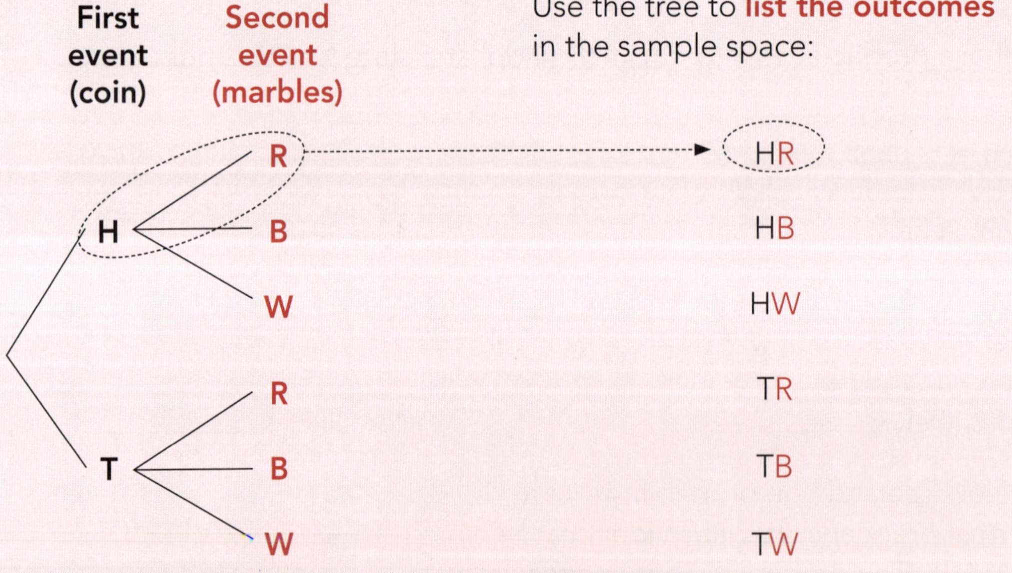

The **number of outcomes** in the sample space is 6.

Another way of calculating the number of outcomes in the sample space:

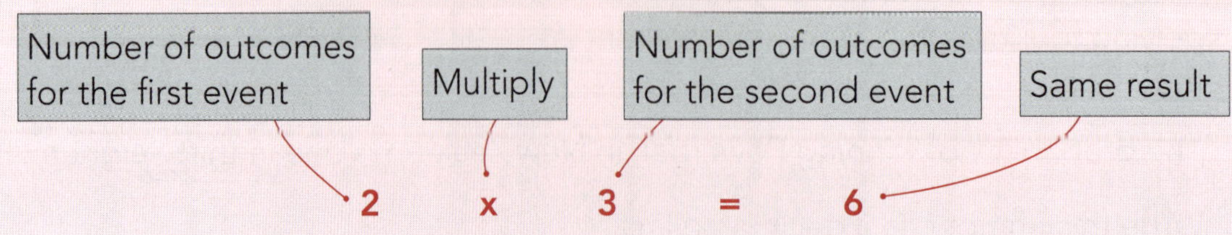

ISBN: 9780170447294

Make a **table**.

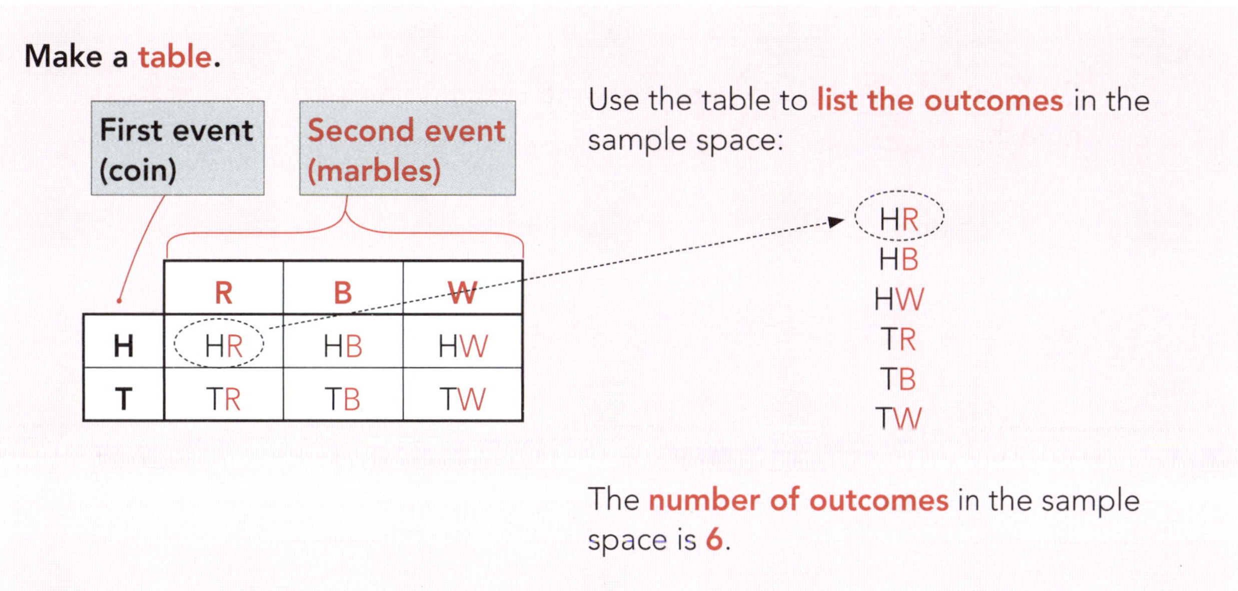

	R	B	W
H	HR	HB	HW
T	TR	TB	TW

Use the table to **list the outcomes** in the sample space:

HR
HB
HW
TR
TB
TW

The **number of outcomes** in the sample space is **6**.

Answer the following.

1 One coin is tossed, then this spinner is spun.

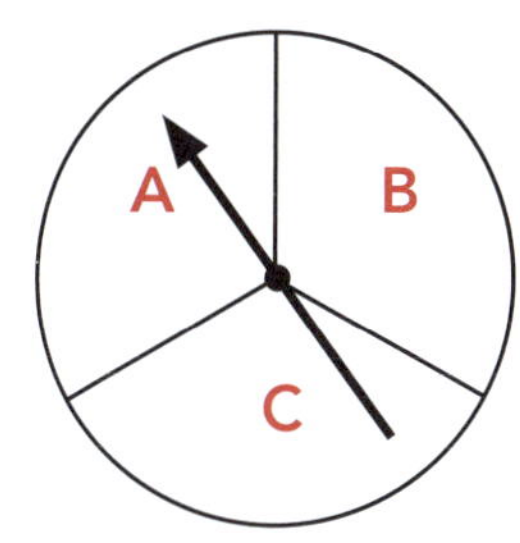

a Complete the probability tree, list the outcomes and write the number of outcomes in the sample space.

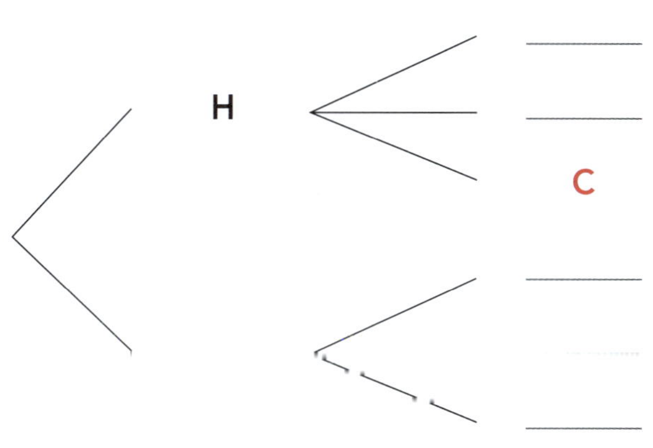

List the outcomes in the sample space:

HA ______________

The number of outcomes in the sample space is ______.

b Complete the table and tick if you get the same result.

	A	B	C
H			
T			

Same result? ☐

c Number of outcomes for the coin = 2

Number of outcomes for the spinner = ______

Multiplying these numbers gives ______

Same result? ☐

ISBN: 9780170447294

2 Some friends need to choose what to eat for dinner. The choices are pizza, burger or sushi, and then after dinner go bowling or to the movies.

a Complete the probability tree and write the outcome at the end of each branch.

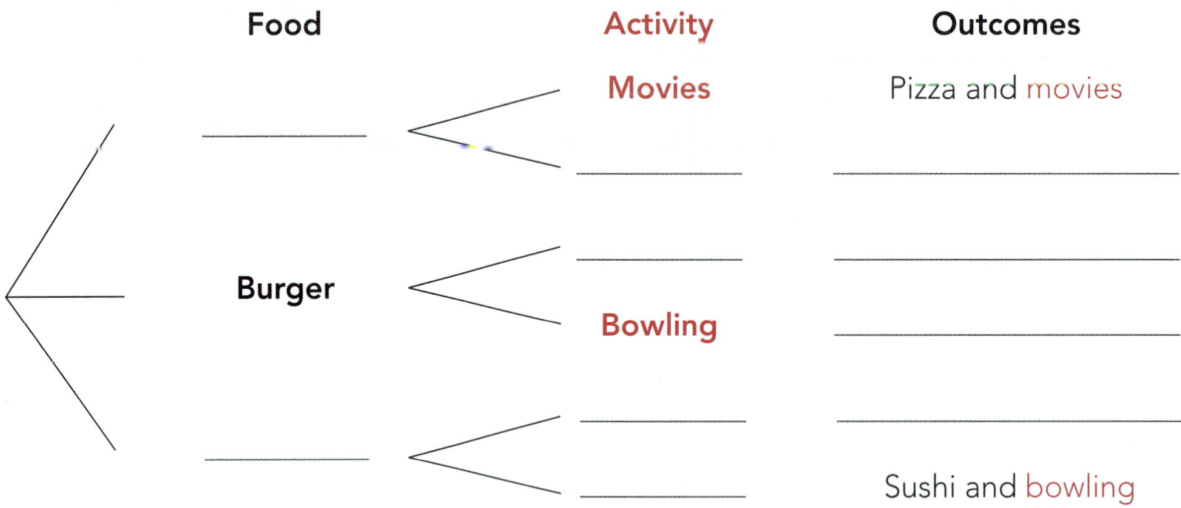

b The number of outcomes in the sample space is ________.

c Complete the table and tick if you get the same result.

		Bowling
Pizza		

Same result? ☐

d number of food x number of activities = _____ x _____
= _____

Same result? ☐

ISBN: 9780170447294

Ways of calculating probabilities

- There are three types of probability: **theoretical**, **experimental** and **actual**.

Theoretical probability — is the probability obtained from a probability model
— can be calculated where there are **equally likely outcomes**.

Note: Unless told otherwise, assume dice, coins etc. are **fair**: they produce **equally likely outcomes**.

e.g. The probability of tossing a coin and getting a head.

Some tools for theoretical probability:

Spinners

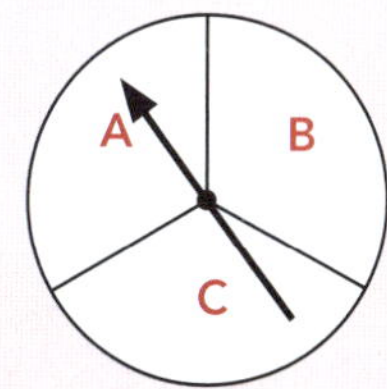

Coins

Dice or die (singular)

Bags of marbles, etc.

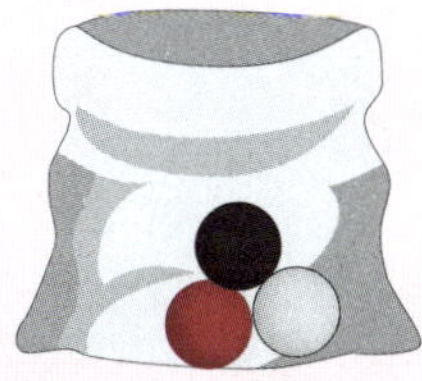

Experimental probability — is the probability obtained from an **experiment** or an **observational study (survey)**
— is calculated using **long run relative frequency**.

e.g. The probability of a red car passing in the next five minutes.

For both of these types:

The number of outcomes we are interested in.

$$\textbf{Probability} = \frac{\textbf{number of 'favourable' outcomes}}{\textbf{number of outcomes in the sample space}}$$

The total number of possible outcomes.

Actual probability — is almost always unknown. It is the actual probability that an event occurs.

e.g. The probability of the bus being late this morning.

Highlight which type of probability applies to these situations.

1	Rolling a six on a die (dice).	Theoretical	Experimental
2	Surveying the class to see who has done their homework.	Theoretical	Experimental
3	Dropping a piece of toast to see if it lands jam-side down.	Theoretical	Experimental
4	Picking a green lolly out of a mixed bag.	Theoretical	Experimental
5	Tossing a coin at the start of a game.	Theoretical	Experimental

ISBN: 9780170447294

Calculating theoretical probability

- When we use devices such as coins, dice and spinners, we **know** the probabilities of single events. We have **equally likely outcomes**.
- We can use these probabilities to calculate the probabilities of combined events.

The number of outcomes we are interested in.

$$\textbf{Probability} = \frac{\textbf{number of 'favourable' outcomes}}{\textbf{number of outcomes in the sample space}}$$

The total number of possible outcomes.

Examples:

1 **One event:** write a **list** of all the outcomes and use it to **calculate probabilities**. e.g. Rolling a die (dice)

a List the outcomes (sample space): 1, 2, 3, 4, 5, 6

b Write down the number of outcomes: 6

c Calculate the probability of rolling a 5: $\frac{1}{6}$

There are **3** even numbers: 2, 4 and 6.

d Calculate the probability of rolling an even number: $\frac{3}{6} = \frac{1}{2}$

There are **4** numbers less than 5: 1, 2, 3 and 4.

e Calculate the probability of rolling a number less than 5: $\frac{4}{6} = \frac{2}{3}$

2 **More than one event:** use **probability trees** and **probability tables** and use them to **calculate probabilities**.

e.g. Picking a marble out of the bag then spinning the spinner

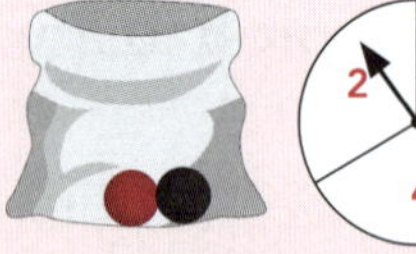

a Calculate the probability of getting a red marble and a 3.

b Calculate the probability of getting a black marble and an even number.

Using a **table**:

	2	3	4
R	R2	R3	R4
B	B2	B3	B4

This means 'The probability of getting a red (marble) and a 3'.

a P(red and 3) = $\frac{1}{6}$

b P(black and even) = $\frac{2}{6} = \frac{1}{3}$

ISBN: 9780170447294

Answer the following.

1 It costs \$5 to spin this spinner. You win the amount the pointer lands on.

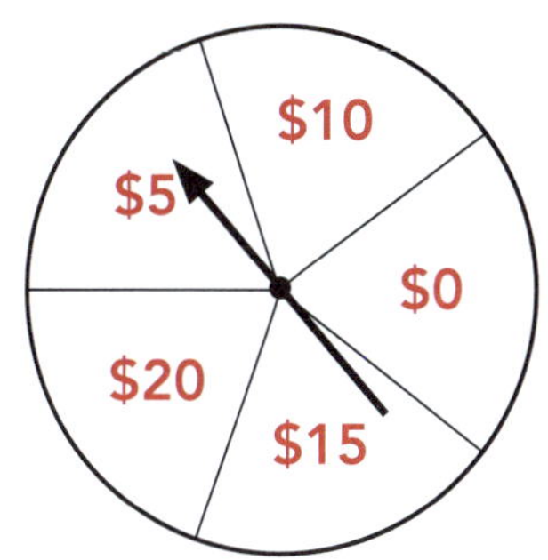

a List the outcomes (sample space):

____

____

b The number of outcomes in the sample space is ________

c What's the probability of getting no money back? ________

d What's the probability of getting at least your money back? ________

e What's the probability of making a profit? ________

f What's the probability of making a profit of \$20? ________

2 A marble is selected from the bag and a die is rolled.

a Complete the table.

				4		
R		R2				
B						
W						

b Number of possibilities in the sample space = ________

c Use the table to help you calculate the following probabilities.

i The probability of getting a black marble and a 5. P = ________

ii The probability of getting a red marble and a 1 or 2. P = ________

iii The probability of getting an odd number. P = ________

iv The probability of getting a black marble and an odd number. P = ________

v The probability of getting a white marble and a 7. P = ________

ISBN: 9780170447294

3 A spinner is spun and a coin is tossed.

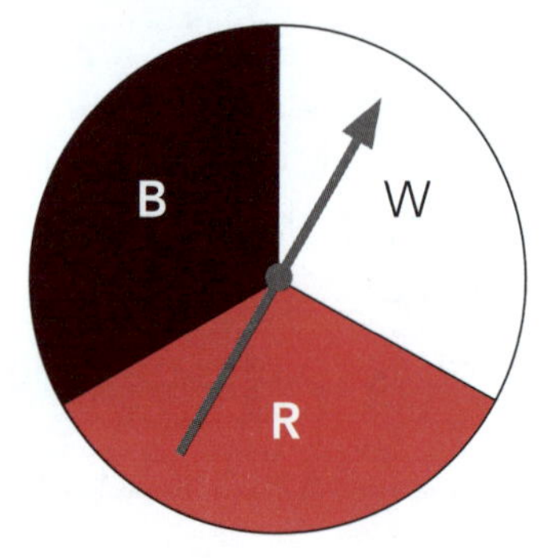

a Complete the tree diagram.

Spinner	Coin	Outcome	Probability
______	H	______	______
	______	RT	P(RT) = ______
B	______	______	______
	T	______	______
______	______	WH	______
	______	______	______

b Number of possibilities in the sample space = ______

c Use the tree to help you calculate the following probabilities.

i The probability of getting a red and a tail. P = ______

ii The probability of getting a white and a head or tail. P = ______

iii The probability of getting a head. P = ______

iv The probability of landing on black. P = ______

v The probability of not getting a red, nor a tail. P = ______

vi The probability of getting a blue and a tail. P = ______

 ISBN: 9780170447294

Challenge 1

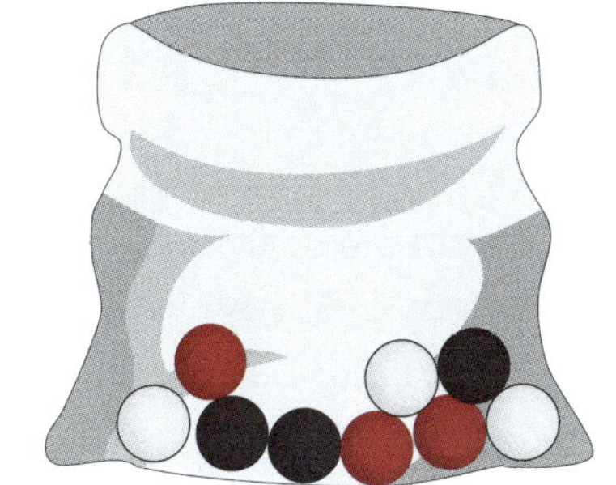

Answer the following questions.

1 There are nine marbles in a bag.

a What is the probability of picking a red marble out of the bag? P = ____________

The red marble is not put back in the bag.

b What is the probability of picking another red marble out of the bag? P = ____________

c What is the probability of picking a white marble out of the bag? P = ____________

d What is the probability of picking a white or a black marble out of the bag? P = ____________

The second red marble is picked and not put back in the bag either.

e What is the probability of picking the third red marble out of the bag? P = ____________

f What is the probability of picking a black marble out of the bag? P = ____________

g What is the probability of picking a white or a black marble out of the bag? P = ____________

2 Kahu has a bag of lollies. It contains 3 mints, 5 fruit bursts and 8 milkshakes. Each time he chooses a lolly, he does it without looking.

a What is the probability that he chooses a fruit burst? P = ____________

b He did get a fruit burst, and he ate it. He chooses a second lolly. What is the probability that it's another fruit burst? P = ____________

c It was a mint, and he ate that too. List the lollies that remain in the bag.

____

d From the lollies remaining in the bag, what is the probability that he chooses a fruit burst? P = ____________

e What is the probability that he chooses a fruit burst or a mint? P = ____________

ISBN: 9780170447294

Calculating probabilities from observations

- Where we do not know the probabilities of events, we can do an **observational study (survey)** (or an **experiment** – see next section).
- Probabilities are calculated using **long run relative frequency**.
- Sometimes it isn't possible to use theoretical probabilities.
  e.g. The probability that your teacher will be late to class.
- In situations like this, we have to **estimate** probabilities based on **surveys**.

$$\textbf{Probability} = \frac{\textbf{number of 'favourable' outcomes}}{\textbf{number of outcomes in the sample space}}$$

Examples:

1 Here are the observations of the teacher's lateness for the last 15 periods.

On time	11
Late	4

The teacher has been late 4 times. Based on this data:

$\therefore$ P(being late to next class) $= \frac{4}{15} = 0.2\dot{6}$ (3 dp)

2 Fifty students at a school were asked what activity they would like to do.

Soccer	**Hockey**	**Netball**	**Orienteering**
16	13	9	12

P(Hockey) $= \frac{13}{50} = 0.26$ P(Orienteering) $= \frac{12}{50} = 0.24$

P(Soccer or Hockey) $= \frac{16}{50} + \frac{13}{50} = \frac{29}{50}$

$= 0.58$

3 A class of students had the demographics below.

	Black hair	**Brown hair**	**Totals**
Year 9	5	8	13
Year 10	9	4	13
Totals	14	12	**26**

P(Black hair) $= \frac{14}{26} = 0.54$ (2 dp) P(Year 10) $= \frac{13}{26} = 0.5$

P(Year 9 and Brown hair) $= \frac{8}{26}$

$= 0.31$ (2 dp)

ISBN: 9780170447294

Answer the following questions.

Win	4
Draw	2
Loss	3

1 The Dolphins water polo team plays the Sharks water polo team each week. These are the results of the water polo team so far this season.

a How many games have they played? ____________

b Based on these results, what is the probability they will win their next game?

P(win) = ____________

c Based on these results, what is the probability they draw or lose their next game? P(draw or lose) = ____________

2 In a class of 28 students, 5 are left handed, 2 are ambidextrous and the rest are right handed.

a What is the probability that a randomly chosen class member is right handed?

P(right handed) = ____________

b What is the probability that a randomly chosen class member is either left handed or ambidextrous? P(left handed or ambidextrous) = ____________

3 On a fishing trip, a number of fish were caught.

Cod	Snapper	Terakihi	Gurnard
8	11	5	2

a How many fish were caught in total? ____________

If you reach into the bin of fish and pull out a fish, calculate the following probabilities.

b P(snapper) = ____________

c P(not a terakihi) = ____________

d P(gurnard or cod) = ____________

4 A survey was done on how 150 students travel to school.

Bus	Car	Walk	Skateboard	Bike
23	51	34	23	19

a What is the probability that a randomly selected student walked to school?

____

b What is the probability that a student walked, skateboarded or biked to school?

____

ISBN: 9780170447294

5 Students went on a school trip and chose to either sail or surf.

a Complete the table.

	Experienced	First time	Totals
Sailing	9	45	
Surfing	14		
Totals			120

b What is the probability that a student went sailing? ____________

c What is the probability that a student was experienced? ____________

d What is the probability that a student was an experienced surfer? ____________

e Which sport had a greater proportion of experienced students? Justify your answer.

____

6 Students can chose to take a language in Year 9 and Year 10.

a Complete the table.

	French	Te Reo Māori	Japanese	Totals
Year 9	34		25	**117**
Year 10	19	43		
Totals		**101**	**46**	**200**

b What is the probability that a language student studied Japanese? ____________

c What is the probability that a language student was in Year 9? ____________

d What is the probability that a student is in Year 9 and studied Te Reo Māori? ____________

e What is the probability that a Year 10 language student takes Japanese? ____________

f What is the probability that a Year 10 language student doesn't take French? ____________

ISBN: 9780170447294

Experimental probability

- Sometimes it isn't possible to calculate probabilities, so we need to carry out **experiments** (or **surveys** — see previous section) in order to estimate them.

1 George thinks that a die is more likely to land on a 6 because it's opposite the 1. He thinks that because there is only one hole drilled into the side with a 1, it is heavier and will land down more often on that side than on the others. Sven disagrees with him.

In order to test this idea, they both decide to do experiments.

George decides to roll a die 10 times and record the result.

These are George's results: **4, 2, 6, 6, 2, 2, 3, 1, 3, 3**.
Here is how he recorded his results:

We call the probability calculated from the results of an experiment, the **experimental probability**.

Die roll	Total	Probability	
1	1	$\frac{1}{10}$	0.1
2	3	$\frac{3}{10}$	
3			
4			
5			
6			

a Complete the table.

b Do you think George's results prove that the probability of getting a 6 is greater than the probability of getting a number other than 6? Yes/No

Explain why or why not.

____

c What do you think George needs to do in order to find out whether his idea is true?

____

d Sven did his own experiment. He rolled a die 50 times. Complete his table of results.

	1	**2**	**3**	**4**	**5**	**6**
Frequency	𝍸 𝍸	𝍸 III	𝍸	𝍸 𝍸 I	𝍸 IIII	𝍸 II
Probabilities	$\frac{10}{50} = 0.2$					

ISBN: 9780170447294

e Do you think Sven's results prove that George's idea was wrong? Yes/No

Explain why or why not.

____

Their teacher decided that it would be good to test George's idea with the whole class. She organised for all 29 students to each roll a die 50 times. Their combined results are shown in this table:

	Total	Probability (4 dp)	
6	231	$\frac{231}{1450}$	
Not 6	1219		

f Complete the table.

g Do you think the class's results prove that George's idea was wrong? Yes/No

Explain why or why not.

____

h Complete the table below to show the probabilities of tossing 6s and not 6s in each of the experiments.

Number of tosses	10	50	1450
P(6)			
P(Not 6)			

What happens to the probabilities as the number of rolls increases?

____

We can assume that dice are manufactured in such a way that they are fair.

i How many 6s would you expect to get if you rolled a fair die a million times?

____

j When George did his experiment, he rolled a die 10 times and these were his results:

4 2 6 6 2 2 3 1 3 3

His last two rolls produced 3s. Tama was watching him and said that if he rolled the die an eleventh time, it probably wouldn't be a 3.

Do you agree with him? Yes/No

Explain why or why not.

____

ISBN: 9780170447294

Complementary events

- **Complementary** events occur when there are **only two possible outcomes**, e.g. scoring a goal or not scoring a goal.
- The probabilities of complementary events **add to 1**.

Notice this is spelt with an '**e**'. Things that are compl**i**mentary are free.

Examples:

1 When tossing a coin, the result must be a head or a tail.

P(head) = 0.5
P(tail) = 0.5 } 0.5 + 0.5 = 1

The events 'tossing a head' and 'tossing a tail' are complementary.

2 Students at your school are either in Year 10 or not in Year 10. So these events are complementary. 23% of the students on the school roll are in Year 10.

∴ P(a student not in Year 10) = 1 – 0.23
= 0.77

3 All the students at a school answered a survey about the length of lunchtime. The options in the survey were: 'It's too long' or 'It's not long enough'.

They found: P(a student thought it was too long) = 0.57
∴ P(a student thought it wasn't long enough) = 1 – 0.57
= 0.43

Answer the following questions.

1 On Sunday, the weather forecast says that the probability of a thunderstorm is 0.2.

The probability that there won't be a thunderstorm = ____________.

2 Students were asked if they had any pets at home. 63% of them confirmed they had at least one pet.

What is the probability that a student doesn't have a pet? ____________

3 Students were asked which of two chocolate flavours they liked best:

P(student liked milk chocolate best) = 0.76

Calculate the probability that a student liked dark chocolate best: P = ____________

= ____________

4 Seventeen students in a class of 29 said they would buy a school magazine.

P(student wouldn't buy a school magazine) = ____________

= ____________

ISBN: 9780170447294

Expected number

Predictions can be made based on probabilities.

Expected number of outcomes = P(event) x number of trials

Examples:

1 The probability of Anna being late to school is 0.06. There are 50 days of school next term. On how many of them would you expect her to be late?

P(late) = 0.06 x 50

= 3

2 Last year the sun was shining on 68% of the days. How many days will we expect the sun to shine this year?

P(sun shining) = 0.68 x 365

= 248.2

We would expect the sun to shine on 248 or 249 days.

Rounding to a whole number is often sensible.

Answer the following questions.

1 Courtney flips a coin 90 times. How many times would you expect it to land on heads? ________

2 The probability of a person being left handed is 0.1. If your school roll is 1423, how many would you expect to be left handed? ________

3 Hemi gets driven to school 24% of the time. How many times in the next 50 days of school can he expect to be driven? ________

4 One in 12 males is colour blind. There are approximately 2.4 million males in New Zealand. How many of them would you expect to be colour blind? ________

5 It has been found that when a team in red plays a team in blue:
P(team in red wins) = 0.75 and P(team in blue wins) = P(draw) = 0.125.
96 such games are played.
How many times would you expect the team in red to win? ________

How many draws and wins for the team in blue would you expect? ________

6 **a** The probability of being born with 11 fingers or 11 toes is 0.002.
The population of New Zealand is 5.084 million.

How many people in New Zealand would you expect to have 11 fingers or toes? ________

b The odds of being injured by a toilet are 1 in 10 000.
How many people in New Zealand would you expect to have been injured by a toilet? ________

ISBN: 9780170447294

Statistical concepts

- It's important to understand some terms and concepts that are important in Statistics.

Census and sample

A census compared with a sample

Census
- You collect data from **every member of the population**.
- You get very accurate information.
- However, it is often impossible and usually very expensive to do.
- It is best to do a census if the answer to the question **really matters**.
- In New Zealand, a census of the population takes place every five years.

Sample
- You collect data from **just some of the population**.
- You don't get such accurate information.
- However, it is much easier and cheaper to take a sample.

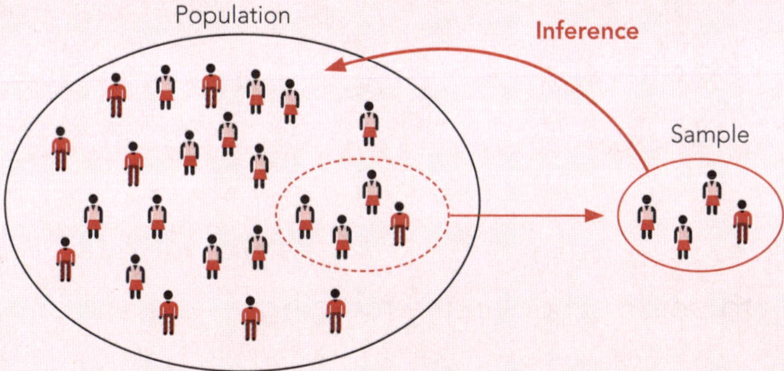

The results from the sample provide an **estimate** or **approximation** about the population. This is known as an **inference**.

Which would be more appropriate for getting information for the following situations, and why?

	Question	Census or sample?	Why?
1	A company wants feedback from customers about their new product.		
2	Do New Zealanders still want to belong to the Commonwealth?		
3	What is the most popular car colour in New Zealand?		

ISBN: 9780170447294

Types of variables

There are three type of variables:

Descriptive variables These are **descriptions** or **names**.
Data recorded about each person/thing: **words**.
Typical question starts with 'What …'
Examples: colour, type of pet, favourite something.

Discrete variables These are **numbers** which are the result of **counting**.
Data recorded about each person/thing: **whole numbers**.
Typical question starts with 'How many …'
Examples: number of pets, number of T-shirts.

Continuous variables These **numbers** are the result of **measuring**.
They can be **fractions** or **decimals**.
Typical question starts with 'How long, heavy, etc. …'
Examples: height, weight, distance, time.

Write down which types of variables these are.

1 Distance to your next class ____________

2 Number of pets ____________

3 Favourite movie ____________

4 Time it takes you to get to school in the morning ____________

Here is some data that has been collected:

Question		Roger	Tama	Elouise
A	How many siblings do you have?	0	2	3
B	How long do you spend watching TV each day?	7 hours	40 minutes	4.5 hours
C	What is your favourite ice cream flavour?	Hokey Pokey	Chocolate	Vanilla
D	How long is your hand?	17.3 cm	15.7 cm	14.9 cm
E	What pet would like to own?	Dog	Cat	Rabbit

5 Which questions have answers that are descriptive variables? ____________

6 Which questions have answers that are discrete variables? ____________

7 Which questions have answers that are continuous variables? ____________

ISBN: 9780170447294

Investigative questions

- There are **three** types of investigative questions.

Summary questions: investigate **one variable** at a time. This could be a word or a number.

Examples: What is your favourite vegetable? — **One variable** — vegetable.

How many pairs of shoes do you have? — **One variable** — pairs of shoes.

Comparative questions: investigate **one variable** for **two groups**.

Example: Did the boys get higher grades than girls in the English test?

One variable — science grade. **Two groups** — girls and boys.

Relationship questions: compare **two variables** for **one group**.

Example: Is there a relationship between height and arm span in Year 10 students?

Two variables — height and arm span. **One group** — Year 10 students.

Write down the type of question these are.

	Question	Type of question
1	What colour are your eyes?	
2	Is there a relationship between the amount of time spent studying and test scores?	
3	How far do you have to walk to get to your letterbox?	
4	Does the fat content of milk affect its boiling temperature?	
5	What is the best TV show you have ever seen?	
6	Do left-handed people write more slowly than right-handed people?	
7	Is the cereal in larger boxes more expensive per gram than that in smaller boxes?	
8	How much did you spend on the shoes you are currently wearing?	
9	Are Year 10 students absent from school more frequently than Year 9 students?	

ISBN: 9780170447294

Data display

- There are different ways of displaying data. Which is most appropriate depends on the **type** of variable:

Descriptive data	Discrete data	Continuous data
Tally chart Pictograph Dot plot Bar graph Strip graph Pie graph	Tally chart Pictograph Dot plot Bar graph Strip graph Line graph/time series Scatter plot Box plot	Histogram Line graph/time series Scatter plot Box plot **If rounded** Dot plot

Write the names of each graph, and the types of data for which each is appropriate.

1

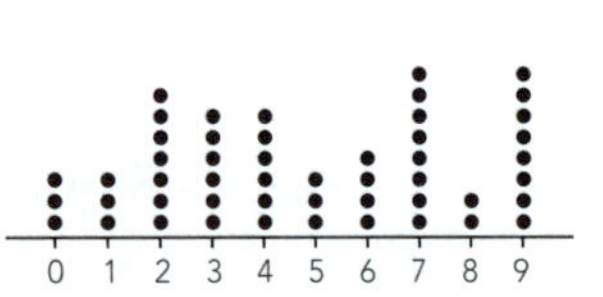

____

____

2

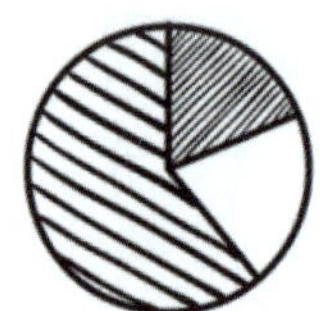

Pie graph

3

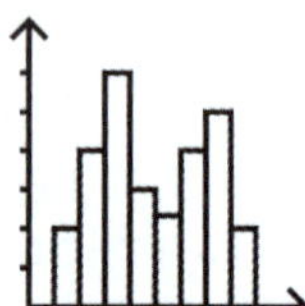

____

____

4

____

____

5

French	||||
German	~~||||~~ ||||
Latin	||
Spanish	~~||||~~

____

____

6

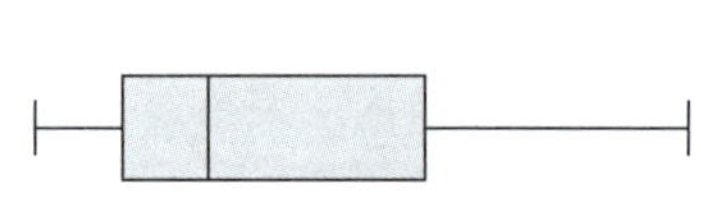

____

____

7

____

____

8

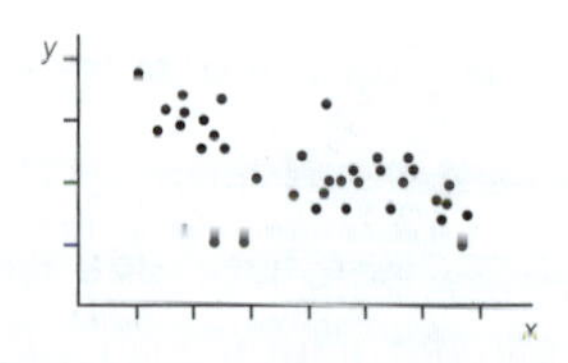

____

____

9

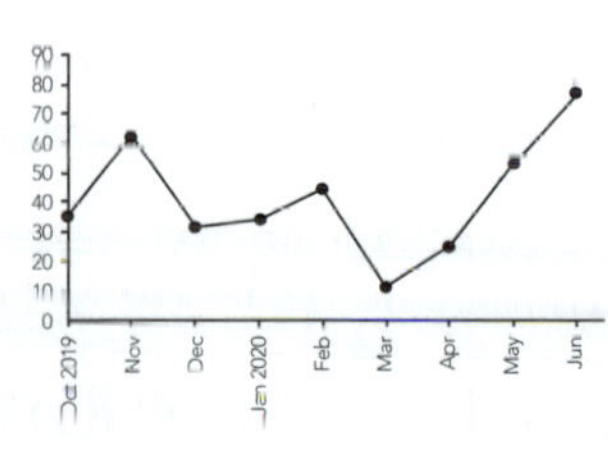

____

____

All sorts of other graphs are used, but remember, fancy doesn't necessarily mean better or easier to understand.

ISBN: 9780170447294

Pie graphs

- Pie graphs are appropriate for **descriptive** data.
- They are best used when there are relatively few divisions of the data.
- The area of each sector is proportional to the frequency of each variable.
- **Single** pie graphs are used to plot the data obtained from answers to a **summative question**.

Understanding pie graphs

Example: A group of students was asked which emoji was their favourite.

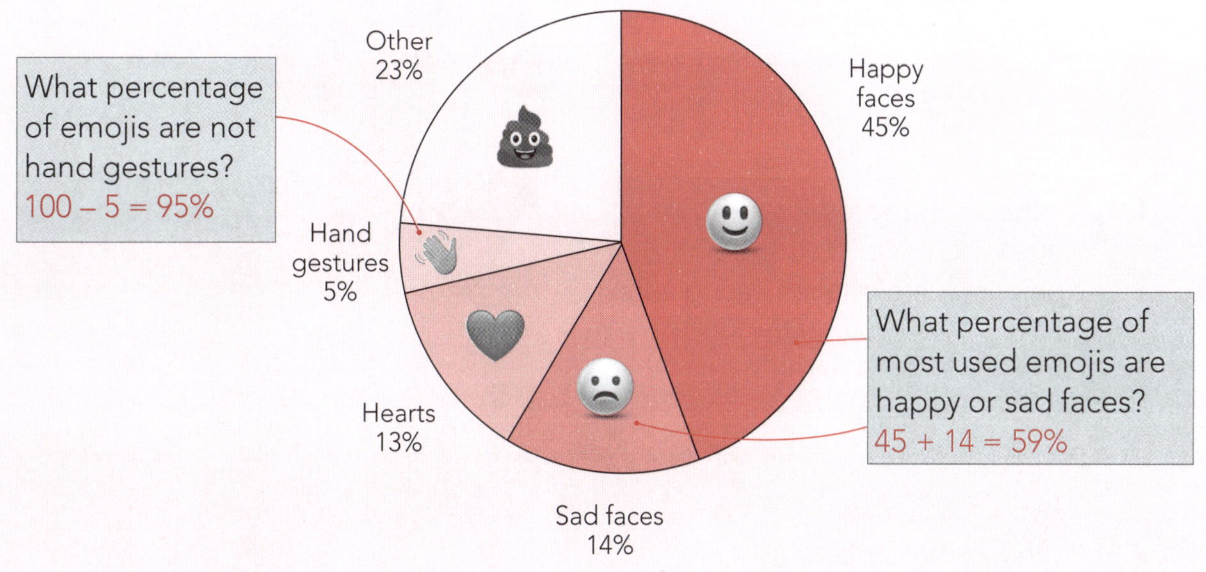

Answer the following questions.

1 The graph shows the ethnicities of the 2020 New Zealand members of Parliament.

a What percentage are not Pākehā? ______________

b A member was randomly selected. What is the probability that they are 'Other'? ______________

c There are 120 members of Parliament. How many Māori members are there?

____

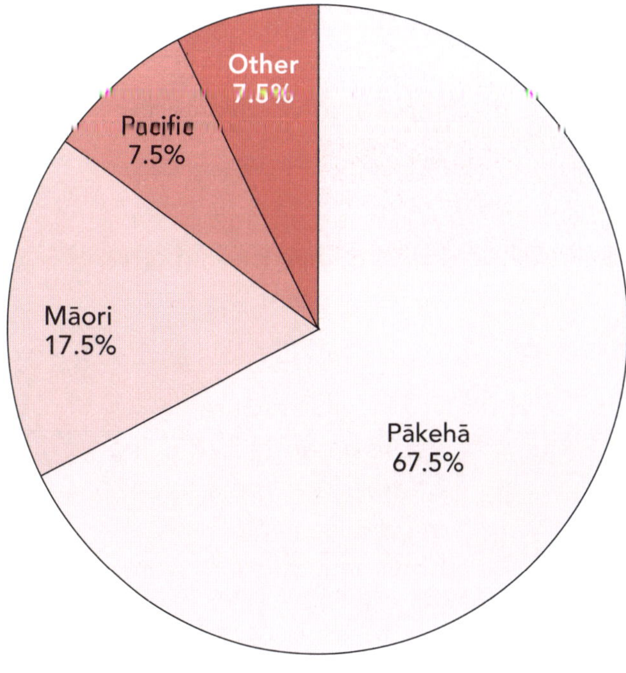

ISBN: 9780170447294

2 The graph shows the New Zealand Bird of the Year votes in 2019.

a Suggest a question that could be asked in order to obtain this data.

b What type of question is this? ______________________________

c How many people voted?

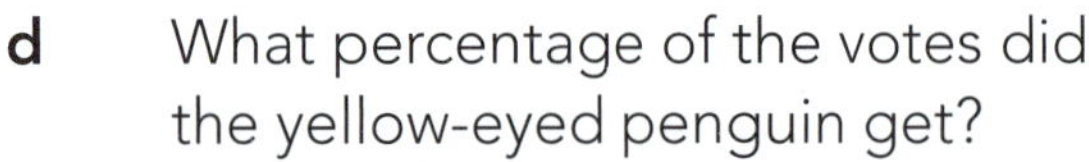

d What percentage of the votes did the yellow-eyed penguin get?

____

e What is the probability that a voter voted for the black robin?

____

f If those who voted for the black robin hadn't voted, what percentage of the remaining votes would have gone to the kākāpō?

____

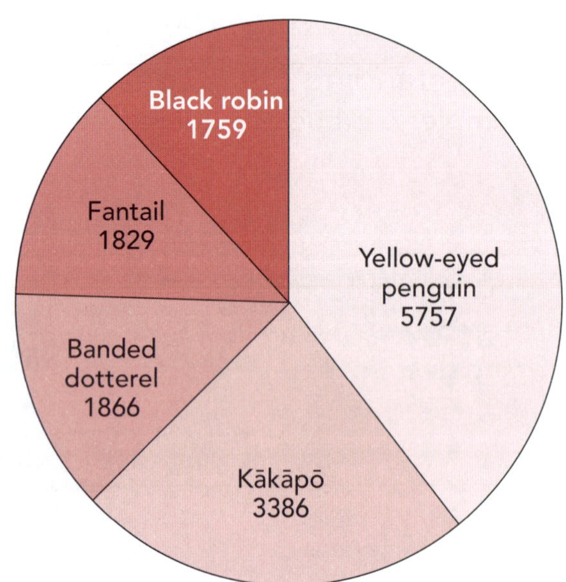

3 The graph shows the marital status of New Zealanders aged 15 years and over in 2019.

a What is the probability that a person has never married?

____

b What percentage of people are currently separated or divorced?

____

c What percentage of people have been married at some point?

d In 2019 there were approximately 3.76 million people over the age of 15 in New Zealand. Estimate how many of them were married.

____

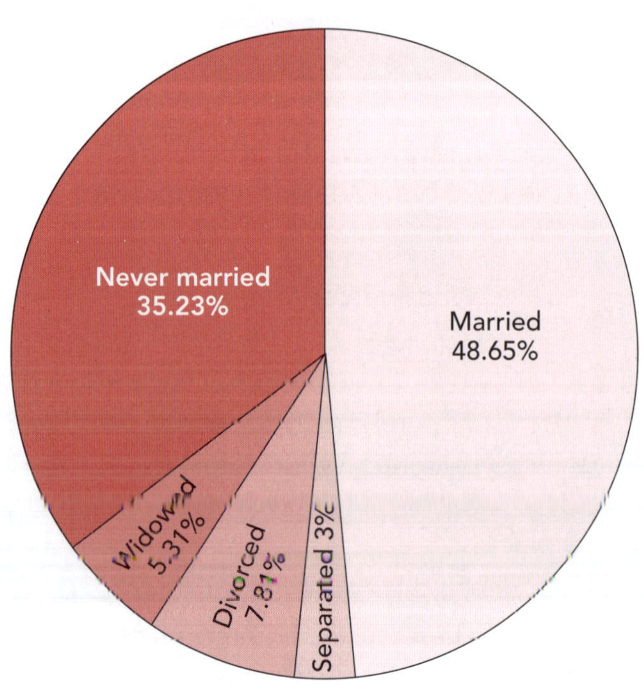

ISBN: 9780170447294

Reading axes

- **Axes** are the horizontal and vertical lines which show the scale.
- The **vertical** axis is the **y**-axis, the **horizontal** is the **x**-axis.

We speak of **one** axis or **several** axes.

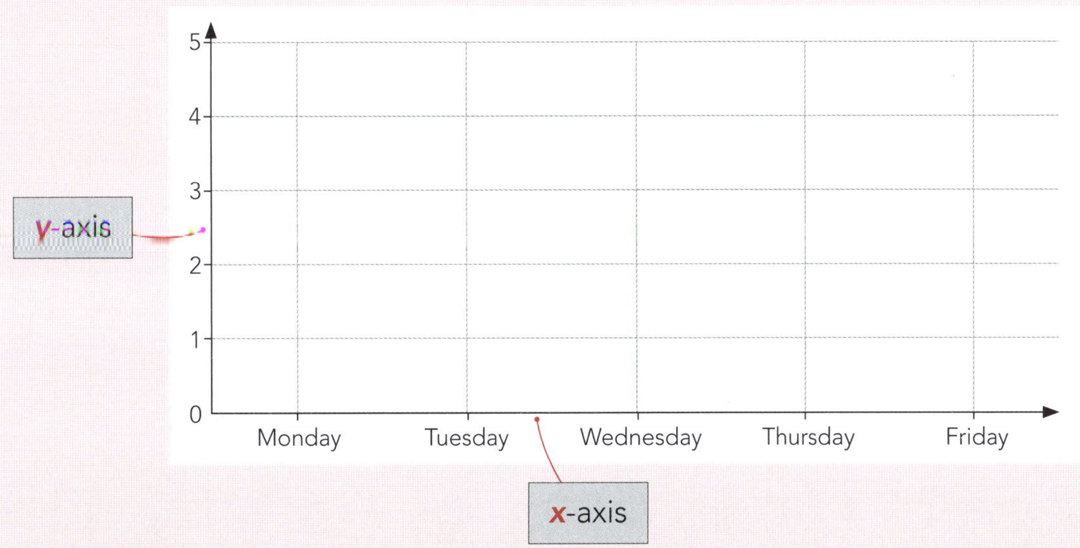

- The gridlines **with numbers** are called '**major**' gridlines.
- The gridlines **without numbers** are called '**minor**' gridlines.
- Look out for multipliers. The axis label may read, for example, '(x 1000)' or '(thousands)'.

Examples:

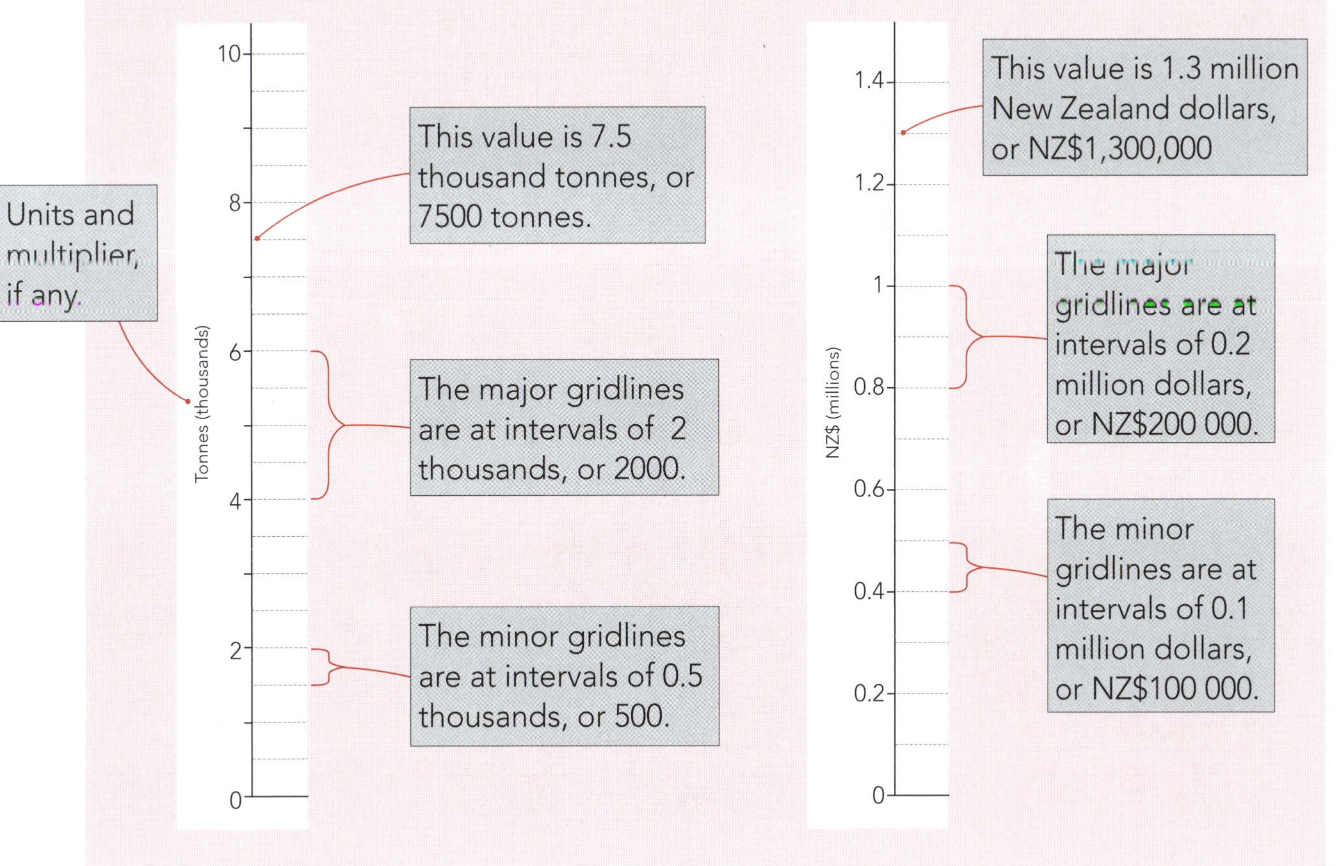

ISBN: 9780170447294

Write down the major and minor intervals, and then fill in the missing values on these axes.

1 Major ________ Minor ________

2 Major ________ Minor ________

3 Major ________ Minor ________

4 Major ________ Minor ________

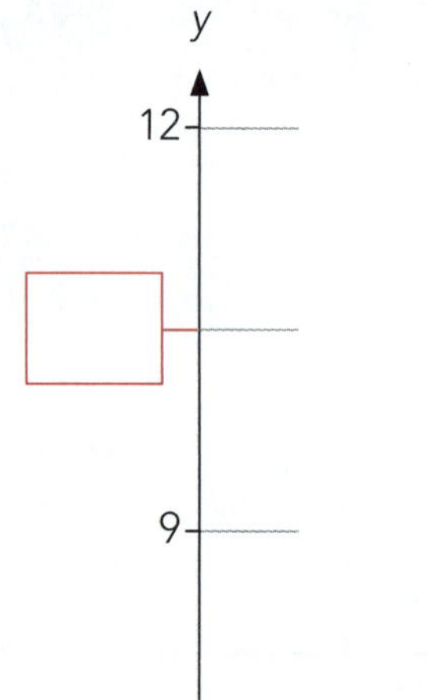
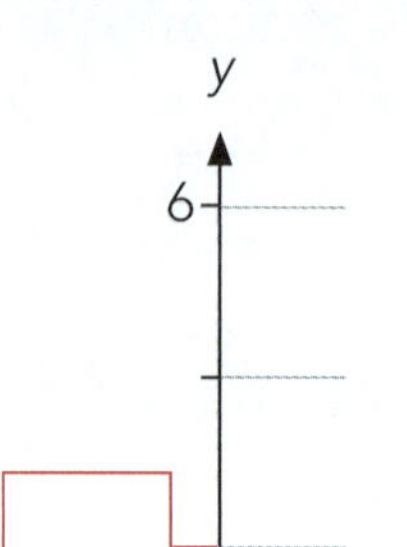
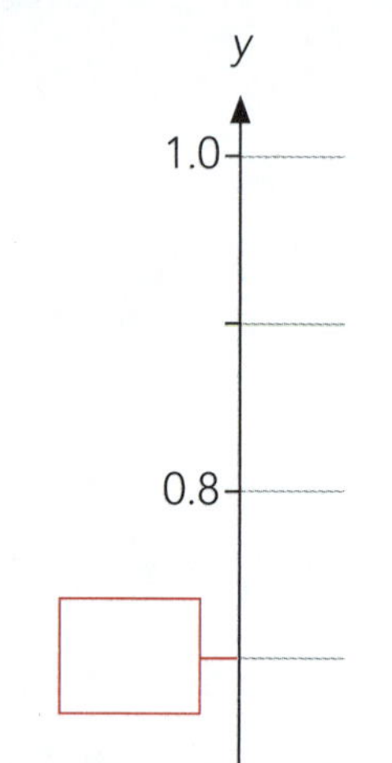
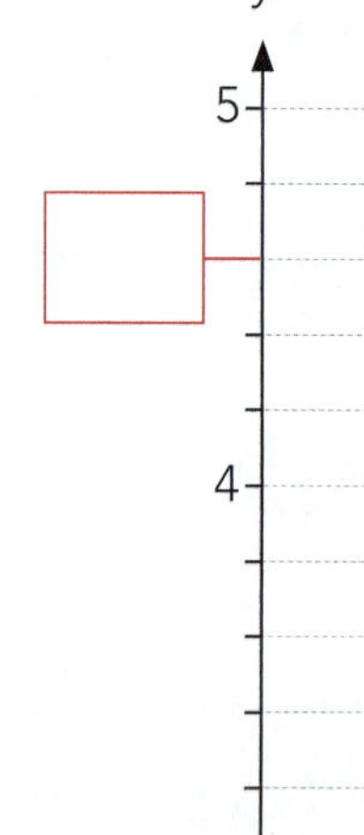
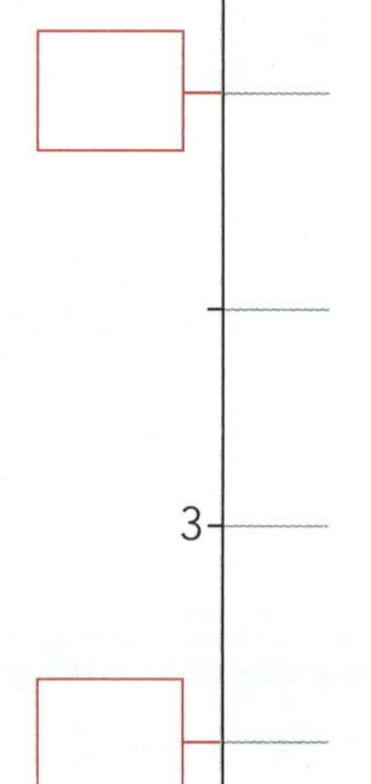
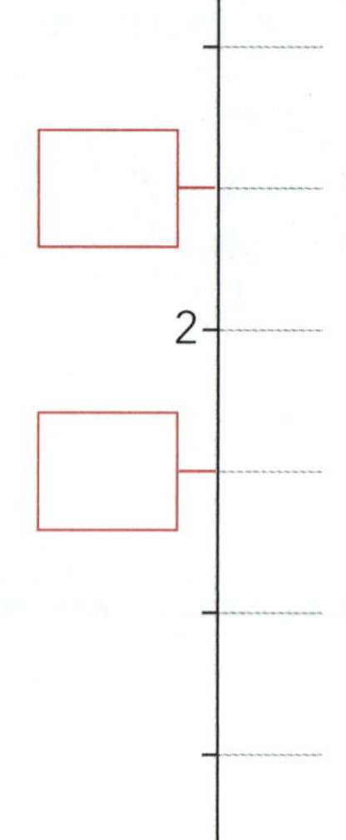
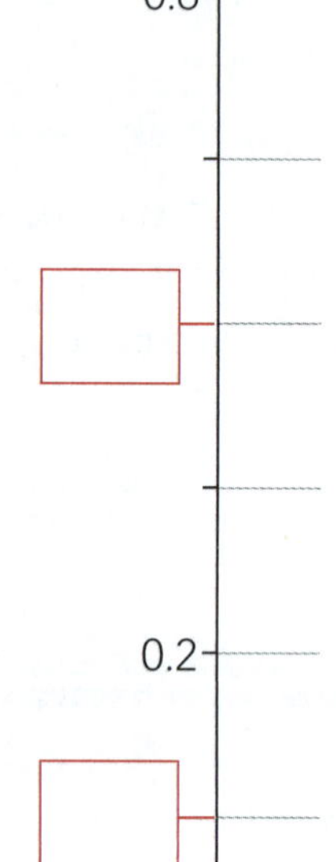
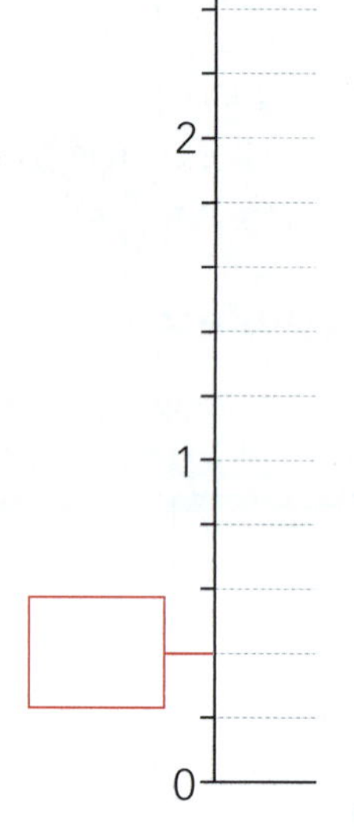

5 Major ________ Minor ________

6 Major ________ Minor ________

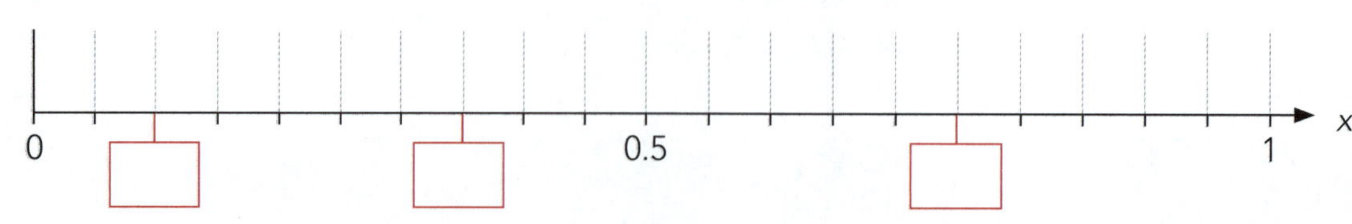

 ISBN: 9780170447294

Write down the values and units represented by each of these points.

7 **8** **9**

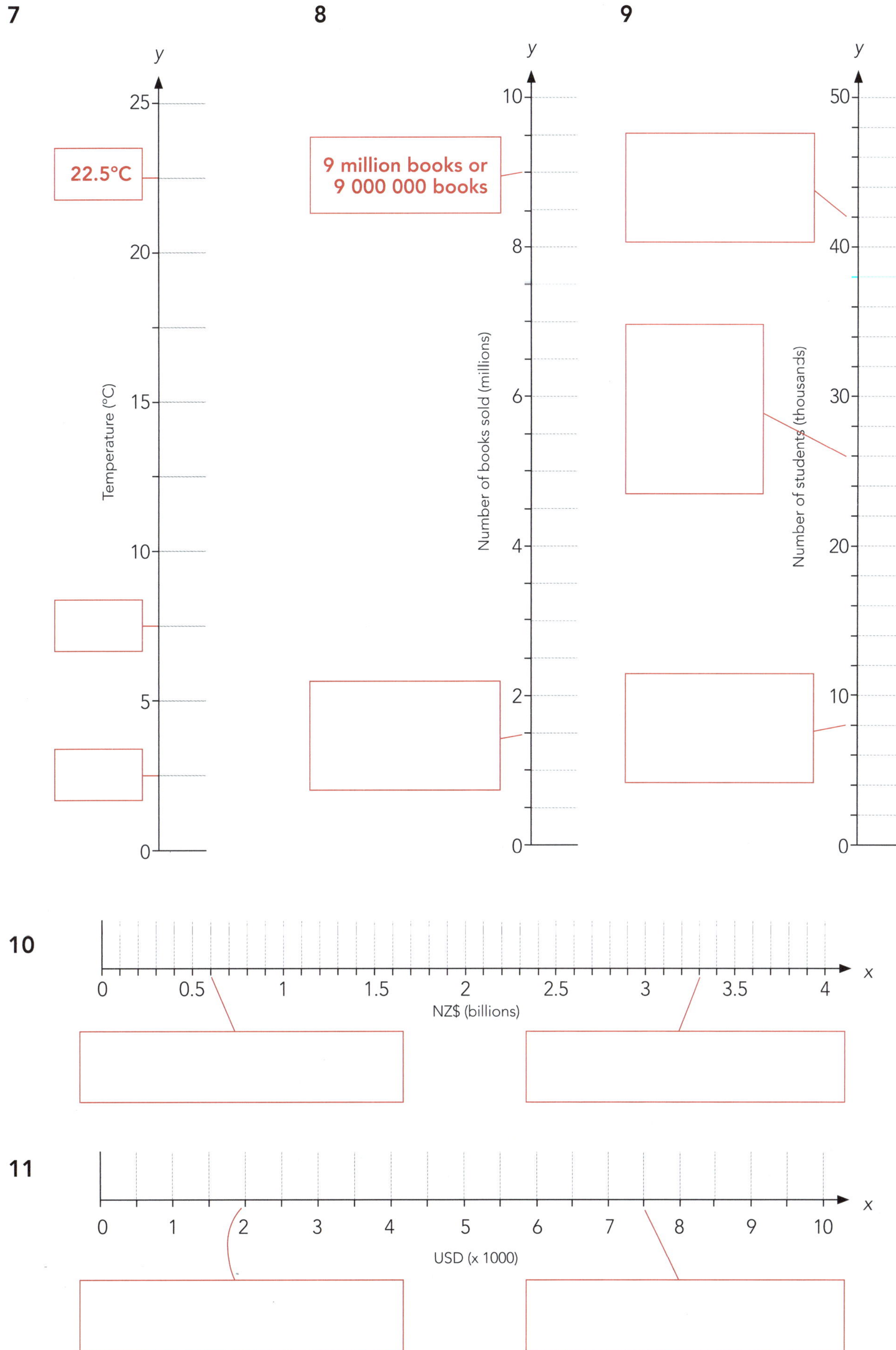

ISBN: 9780170447294

Bar graphs

- Bar graphs are used to display **discrete** or **descriptive** data.
- They are sometimes known as column graphs.
- They can be plotted **vertically** or **horizontally**.
- The bars always have **gaps** between them.
- **Single** bar graphs are used to plot the data obtained from answers to a **summative question**.
- **Double** bar graphs are used to plot the data obtained from answers to a **comparative question**.

Understanding bar graphs

Examples:

1 This graph shows the values of five of New Zealand's largest exports during 2015.

2 Some bar graphs are used for comparison rather than for reading values.

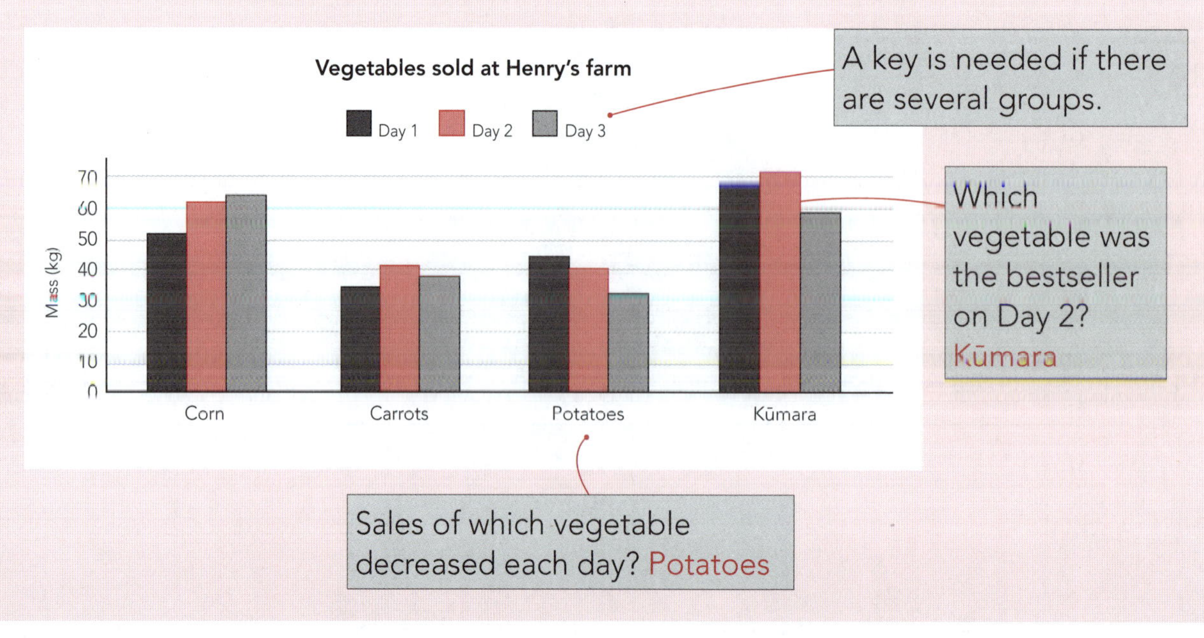

ISBN: 9780170447294

Answer the following questions.

1 The graph shows the estimates of the numbers of each kiwi species in New Zealand.

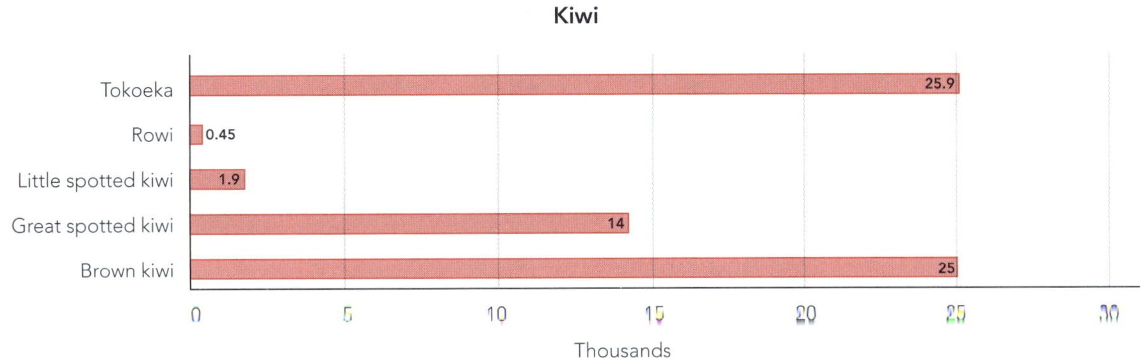

a What is the population estimate for the great spotted kiwi? ______

b How many more tokoeka are there estimated to be than rowi? ______

c What percentage of kiwi are estimated to be little spotted kiwi? Round your answer to 1 dp. ______

2 The graph shows estimates of the number of New Zealand children who brush their teeth twice or more a day.

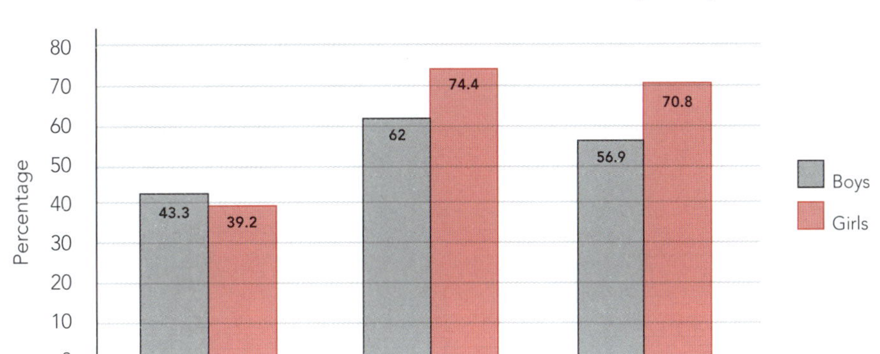

a What percentage of boys aged 5–9 brush their teeth twice or more a day? ______

b What percentage of girls aged 0–4 don't brush their teeth twice or more a day? ______

c Boys aged 10–14 years brush their teeth more often than girls of the same age.

☐ Agree ☐ Disagree ☐ Can't tell for sure

Explain your answer.

______

3 Data on fuel type were collected for red, black, grey and white cars in a carpark.

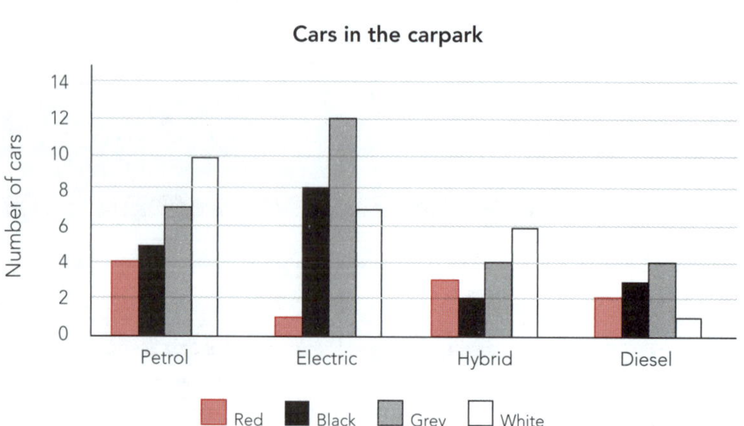

a What's the most common colour of petrol car in the carpark? ____________

b How many cars were electric and white? ____________

c How many black cars were in the carpark? ____________

d Most grey cars were electric.

☐ Agree ☐ Disagree ☐ Can't tell for sure

Explain your answer.

____

4 This graph shows the four most successful countries' medal hauls at the Tokyo Olympics.

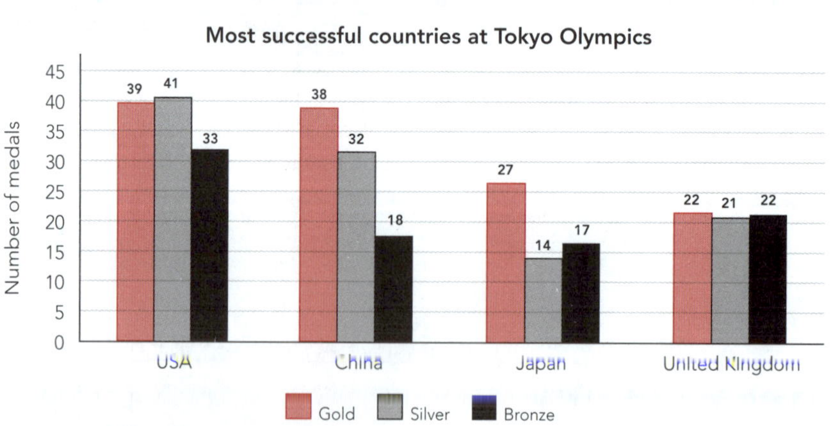

a Which country won the most gold medals? ____________

b How many medals did the UK win in total? ____________

c Which country won more than twice as many gold as bronze medals? ____________

d Which of these countries won the fewest medals in total? ____________

ISBN: 9780170447294

5 The graph shows the numbers of male and female members of Parliament elected in New Zealand between 1931 and 2020.

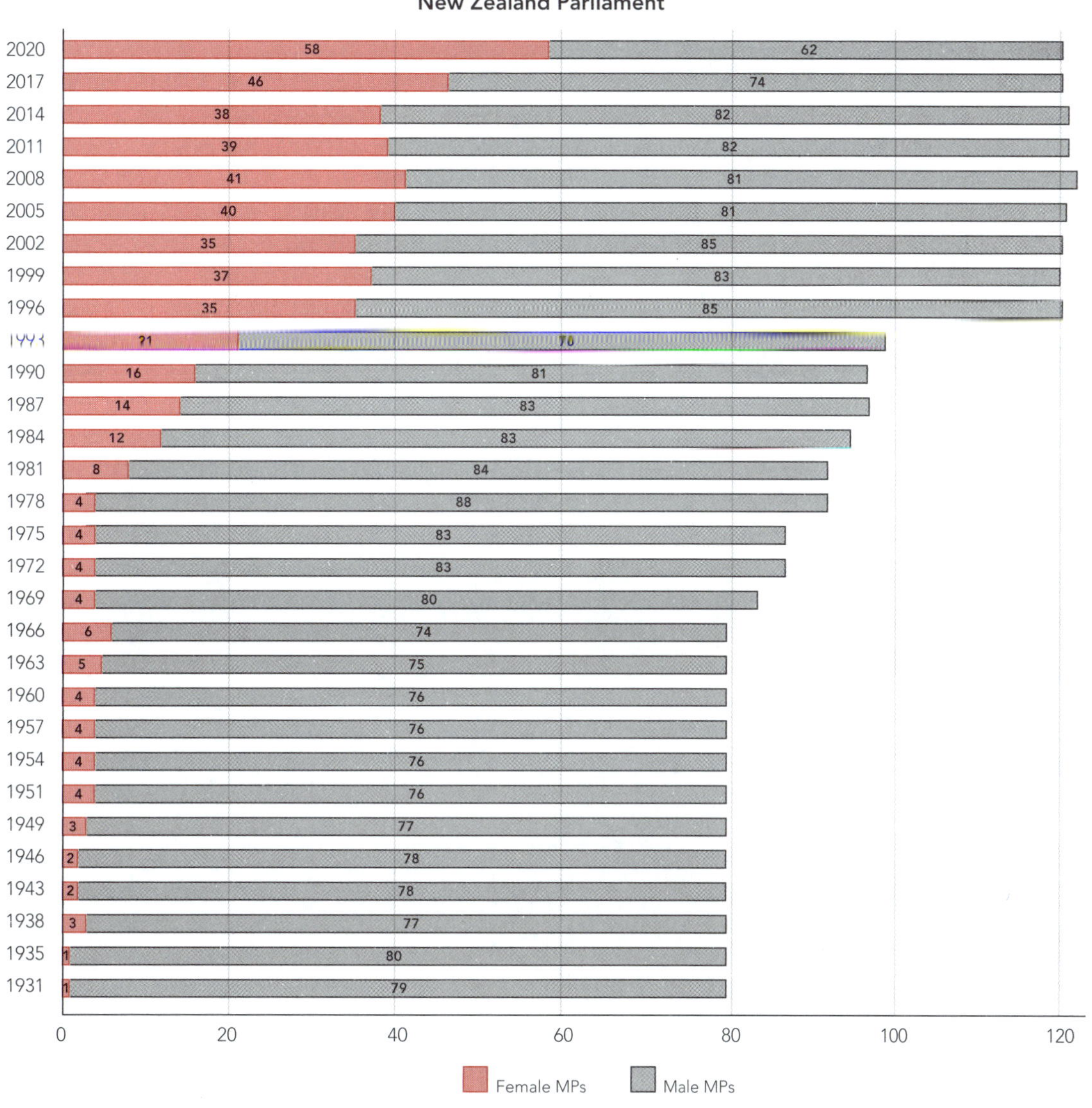

a Suggest a question that this data could be used to answer.

____

b What type of question is this? __________

c How many females were in Parliament in 1993? __________

d When did the total number of members of Parliament first increase? __________

e How many members of Parliament were there in 2020? __________

f What percentage of parliamentarians were females in 1957? __________

In 2020? __________

ISBN: 9780170447294

Line graphs

- Line graphs are often used to show how **discrete** or **continuous** data changes at regular intervals of time.
- Lines connect the plotted points.
- When time is on the x-axis, these are called **time series** graphs.
- **Single** line graphs are used to plot the data obtained from answers to a **summative question**.
- **Double** line graphs are used to plot the data obtained from answers to a **comparative question**.

Understanding line graphs

Examples:

1

Number of lightning strikes in New Zealand

Number of strikes: 0, 50 000, 100 000, 150 000, 200 000, 250 000, 300 000, 350 000

Years: 2008, 2009, 2010, 2011, 2012, 2013, 2014, 2015, 2016, 2017

Estimate the total number of lightning strikes in 2009 and 2010.
220 000 + 130 000 = 350 000

Which year had the fewest lightning strikes?
2012, because this is the lowest point on the graph.

2 There can be several lines on one graph.
This graph shows annual New Zealand imports and exports of ice cream.

What was the difference in imported and exported ice cream in 2019?
12.6 – 7.2 = 5.4 million kg

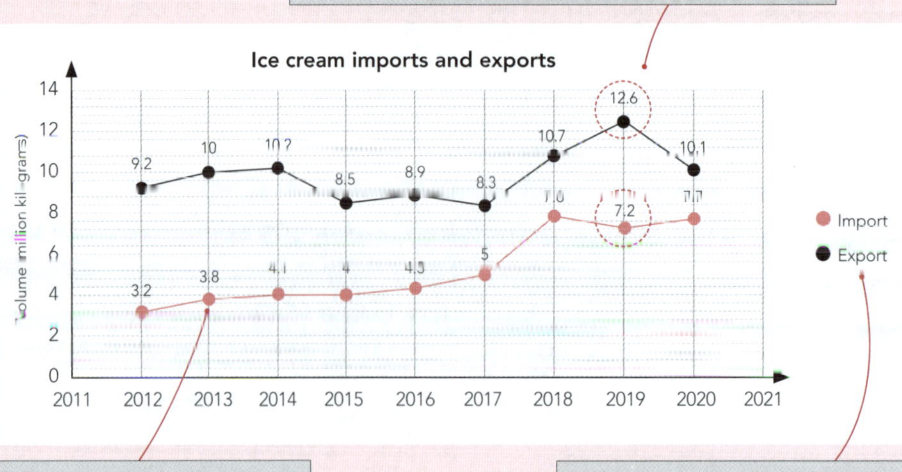

How much ice cream was imported in 2013? 3.8 million kg

A **key** is needed if there are several lines.

 ISBN: 9780170447294

1 The graph shows the percentage of New Zealand children (aged 2–14) who meet fruit intake guidelines.

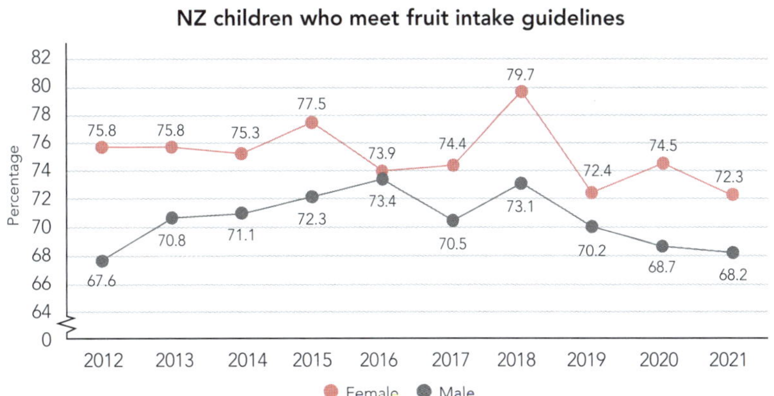

a What percentage of females were reaching the fruit guidelines in 2017? ________________

b What's the lowest percentage that male children have reached? ________________

c Which year was there the biggest gap between male and females? ________________

d If you were checking this data, which value would you be most suspicious about, and why?

____

2 These are the average monthly temperatures for three New Zealand locations.

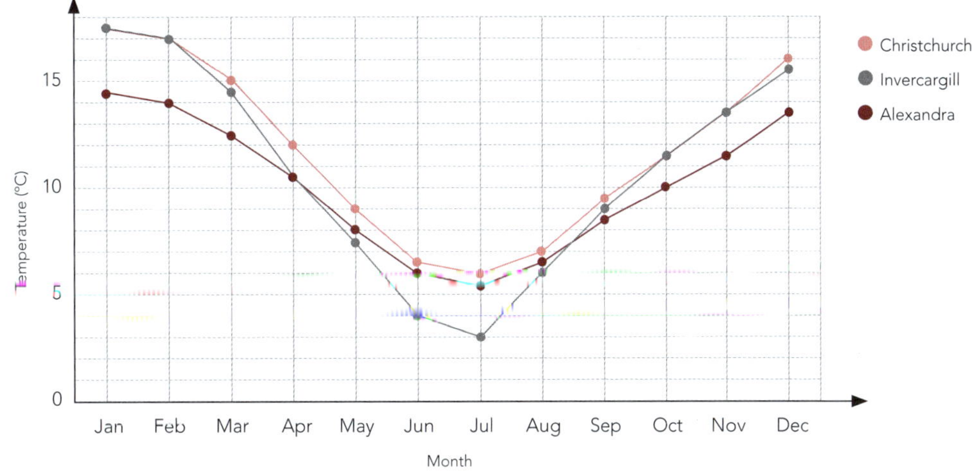

a What is the average temperature in Christchurch in May? ________________

b In which month is Invercargill's average temperature 8.5°C? ________________

c Estimate the difference between the average temperature of Alexandra and Invercargill in July. ________________

d Which location has the most variable temperatures? ________________

ISBN: 9780170447294

3 The graph shows the prices of three food items between 2012 and 2022.

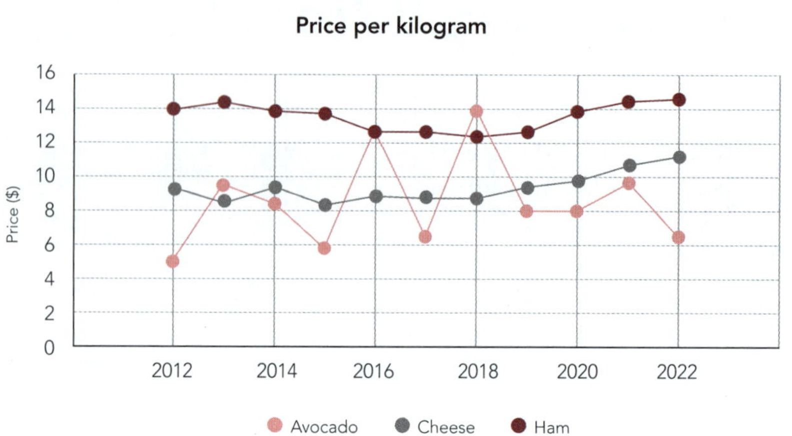

a Suggest a question that could be asked in order to obtain this data.

____

b What type of question is this? ______________

c Estimate the price of ham per kilogram in 2012? ______________

d In which year was avocado and ham the same price? ______________

e In which year were avocados more expensive than both ham and cheese? ______________

f Which food had the most variable prices? ______________

4 The graph shows babies born in New Zealand with the names Sophia, Mia and Hannah.

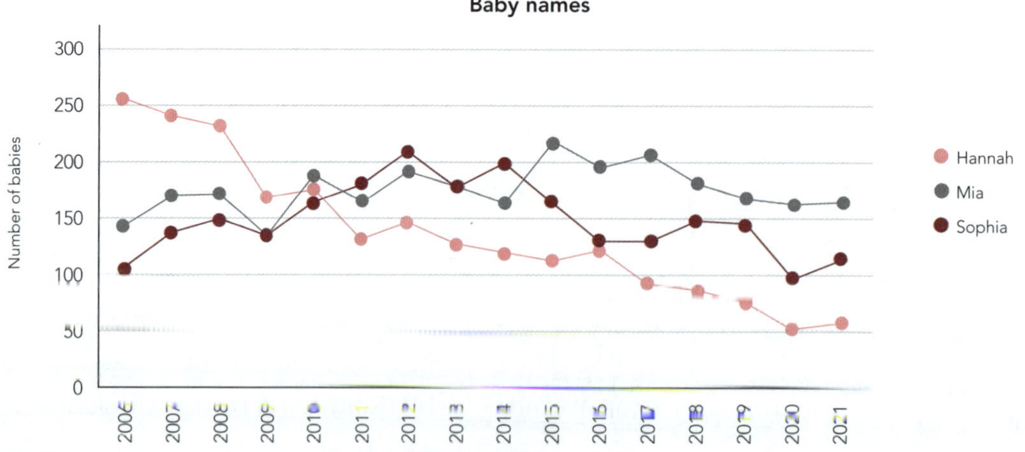

a Which name has decreased most in popularity over the last 20 years? ______________

b Which year saw all three names similar in popularity? ______________

c Which of the three names was most popular in 2021? ______________

 ISBN: 9780170447294

Histograms

- Histograms are used to display **continuous** (**measured**) data.
- The data is displayed in **intervals**.
- There are **no gaps** between the bars.
- Histograms are used to plot the data obtained from answers to a **summative question**.

Understanding histograms

Example: Students' bank balances are graphed below.

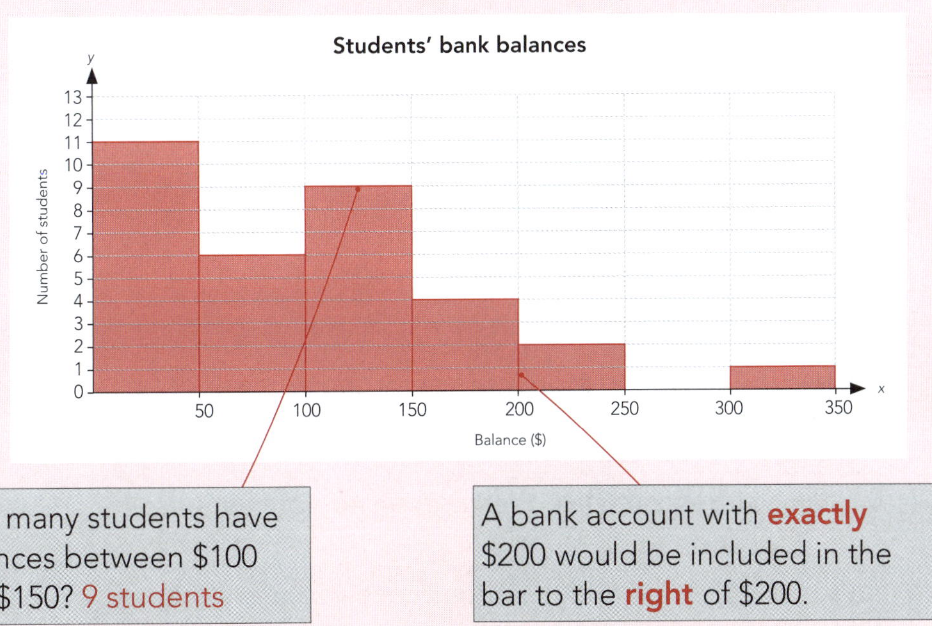

Answer the following questions. Round any calculations to 3 sf.

1 Below is the distribution of ages of 896 Nobel Prize recipients.

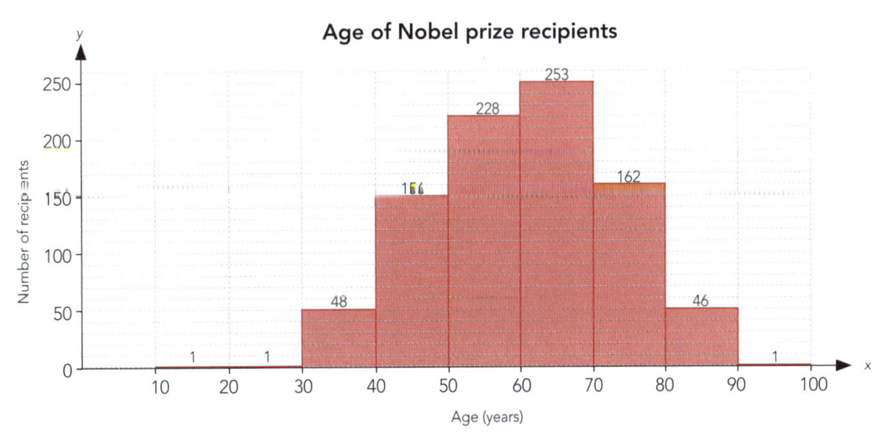

a What is the most common age interval of recipients? __________

b Exactly forty-six recipients were in which age interval? __________

c What is the probability of a Nobel Prize recipient being between 40 and 50 years old? __________

ISBN: 9780170447294

2 A class was asked 'How many notifications did you receive during the last 60-minutes?'

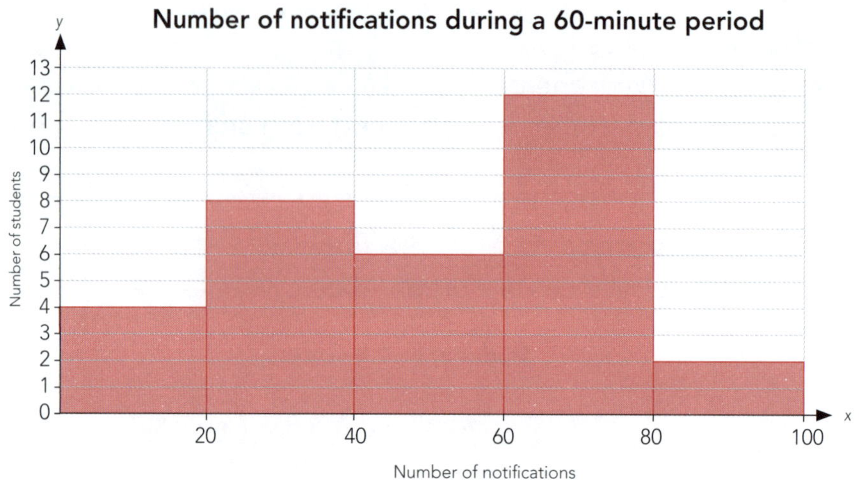

a What type of question is this? __________

b How many students received between 40 and 60 notifications? __________

c What was the most common interval for the number of notifications? __________

d How many students received fewer than 40 notifications? __________

e What's the probability that a student received more than 80 notifications? __________

3 The graph shows the 2020 Tokyo Olympics men's marathon times.

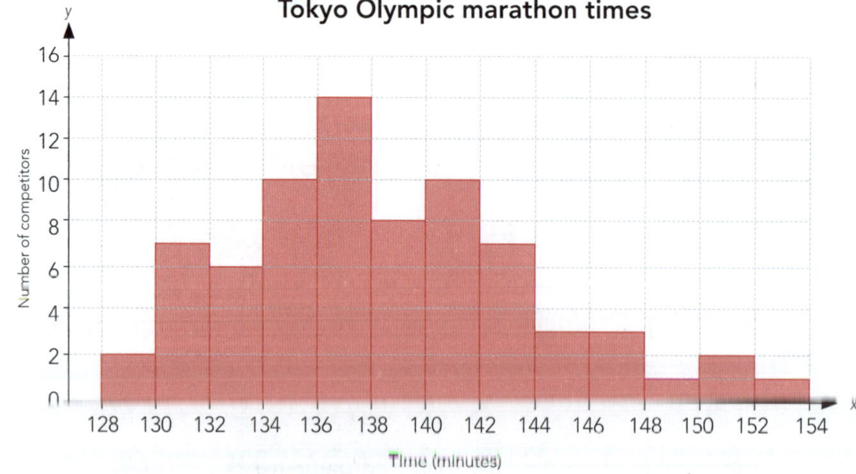

a In what interval was the winning time for the marathon? __________

b How many runners took between 130 and 132 minutes? __________

c How many runners took more than two and a half hours? __________

ISBN: 9780170447294

Dot plots

- Dot plots are used for **discrete** and **rounded continuous** data.
- They are useful for **comparing groups**.
- Each dot represents one person/object, unless you are told otherwise.
- **Single** dot plots are used to plot the data obtained from answers to a **summative question**.
- **Pairs** of dot plots are used to plot the data obtained from answers to a **comparative question**.

Examples:

1 A group of students were asked to record how many hours (to the nearest hour) they spent on their phone in a day (over 24 hours).

How many students spent more than three hours on their phone?
4 students, because there are 4 dots to the right of three hours.

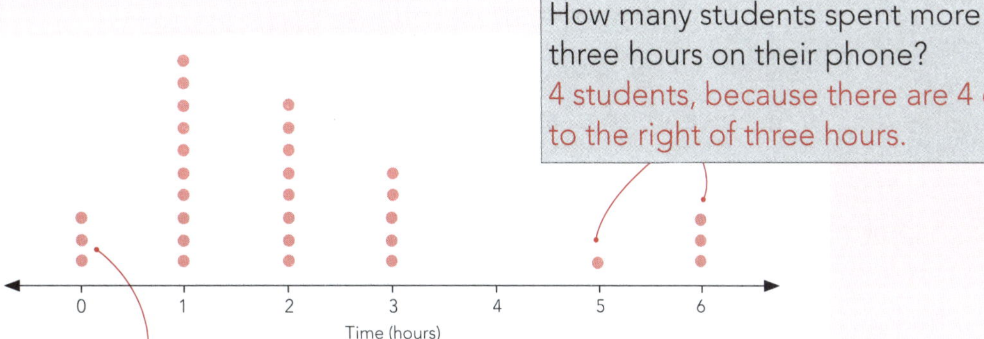

What is the probability that a student spent no time on their phone? $\frac{3}{30} = 0.1$

Dot plots can be useful for comparing data sets.

2 Height of Year 9 and 10 students.

Year 10

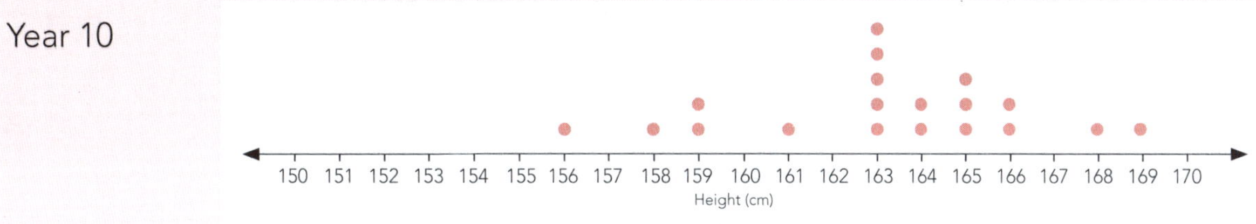

Year 9

150 151 152 153 154 155 156 157 158 159 160 161 162 163 164 165 166 167 168 169 170
Height (cm)

Suggest a question that this data could be used to answer.
What is the difference between the heights of Year 9 students and Year 10 students?

What type of question is this? Comparative

Which year group is taller? Year 10 are taller.

Explain your answer. There are more dots towards the right of the Year 10 graph, which means that the students in this year group are taller.

ISBN: 9780170447294

1 Students were asked 'How many countries other than New Zealand have you visited?'

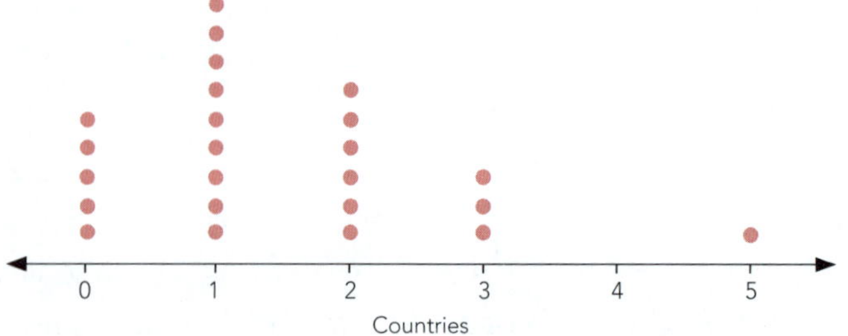

a What type of question is this? ______________

b How many students have visited just one country? ______________

c How many students have visited more than two countries? ______________

d What is the probability that a student hasn't left New Zealand? ______________

e What percentage of students have visited two or three countries? ______________

2 Below are the heights of some Tall Blacks and All Blacks.

Tall Blacks

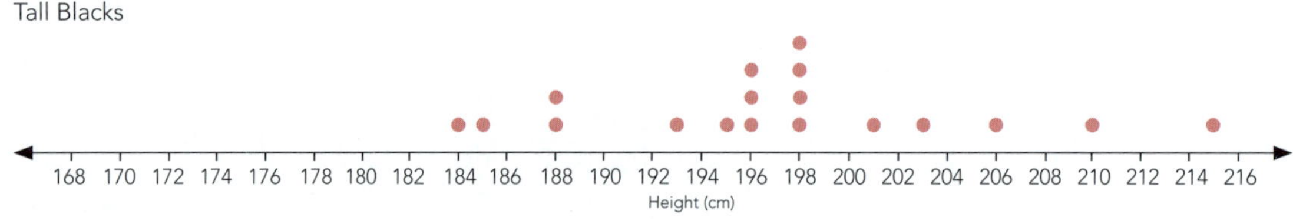

All Blacks

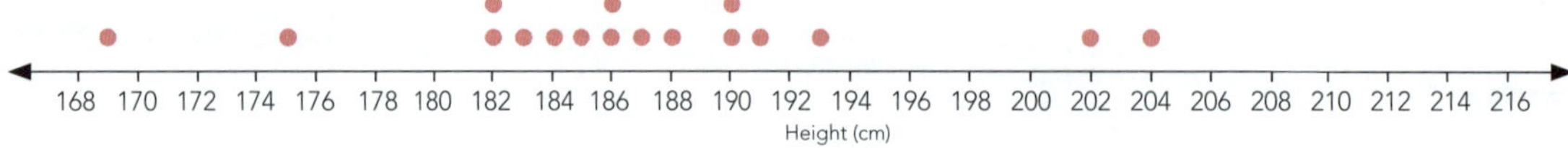

a How many Tall Blacks are more than 2 m tall? ______________

b What is the most common height of Tall Blacks? ______________

c Which sport has the taller players? ______________

How do you know? ____

d What is the probability of an All Black being more than 2 m? ______________

e Most All Blacks are between 180 cm and 200 cm tall.

☐ Agree ☐ Disagree ☐ Can't tell for sure

Explain your answer. ____

____

 ISBN: 9780170447294

Describing features of dot plots

Spread

This can be calculated or compared.

Shape

If samples are large enough, you may be able to comment on the shape.
None will be perfect, so use the term '**tends towards**'.

Bell shaped/normal distribution Symmetrical hill or mound shape	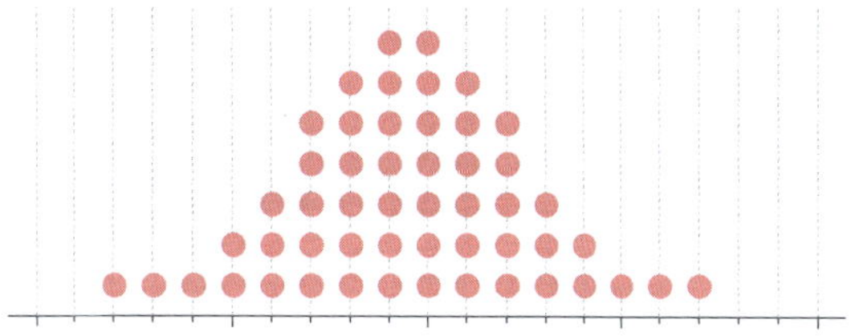
Skewed to the right The tail is on the right-hand side.	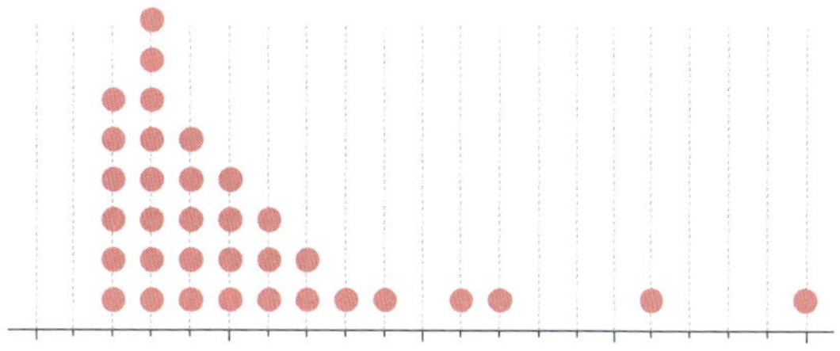
Skewed to the left The tail is on the left-hand side.	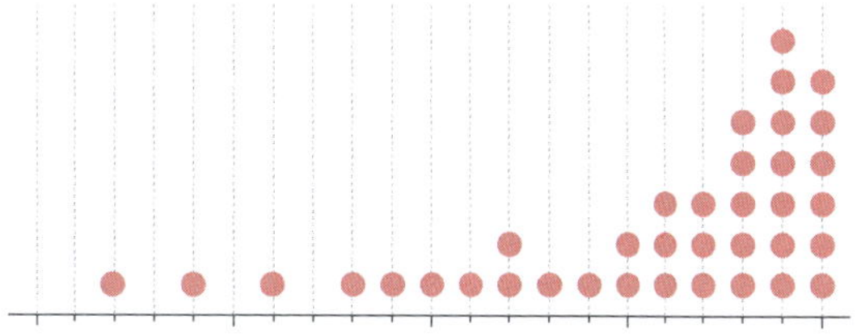
Irregular There is no real pattern.	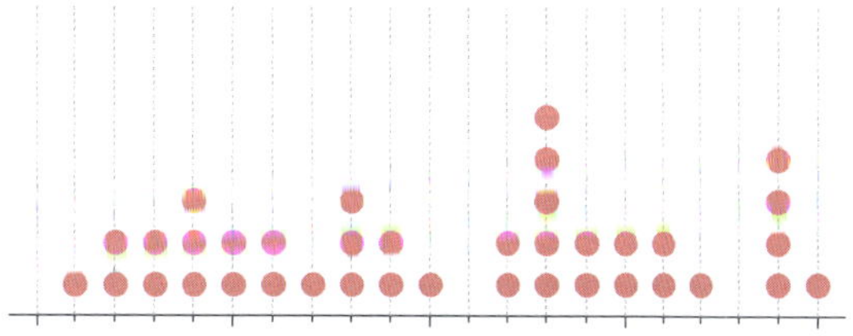

Highlight the shape that these graphs tend towards.

3

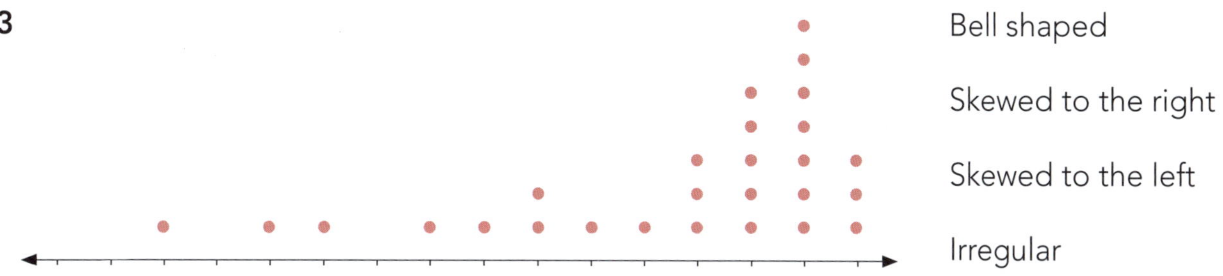

Bell shaped

Skewed to the right

Skewed to the left

Irregular

ISBN: 9780170447294

4

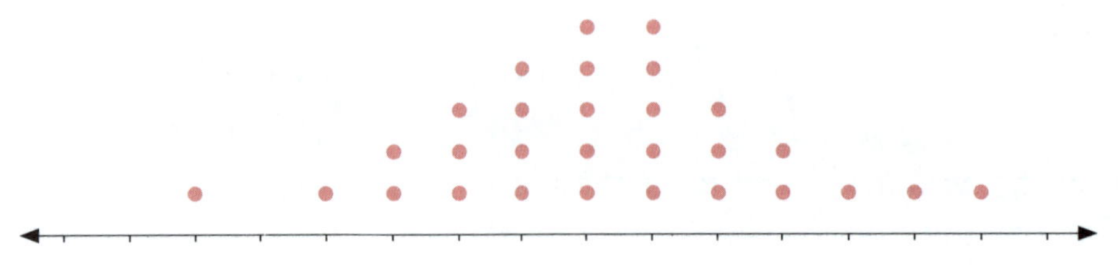

Bell shaped

Skewed to the right

Skewed to the left

Irregular

5

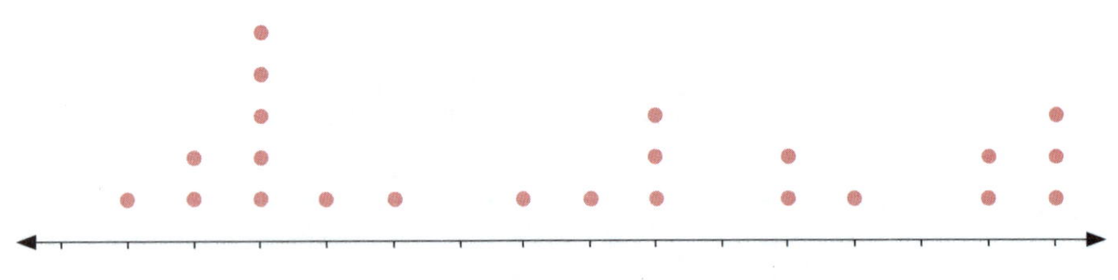

Bell shaped

Skewed to the right

Skewed to the left

Irregular

6

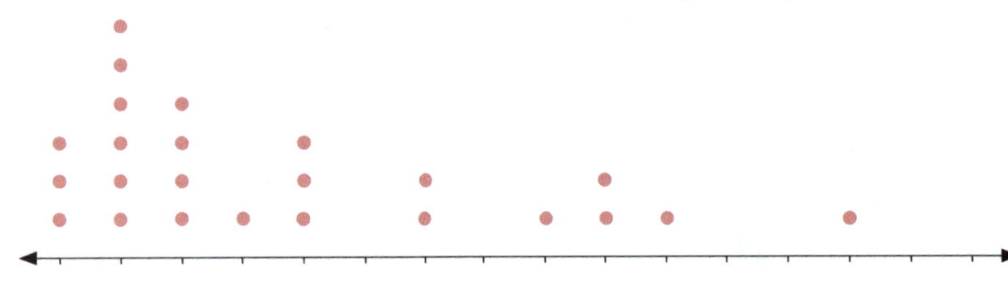

Bell shaped

Skewed to the right

Skewed to the left

Irregular

7 Compare these distributions.

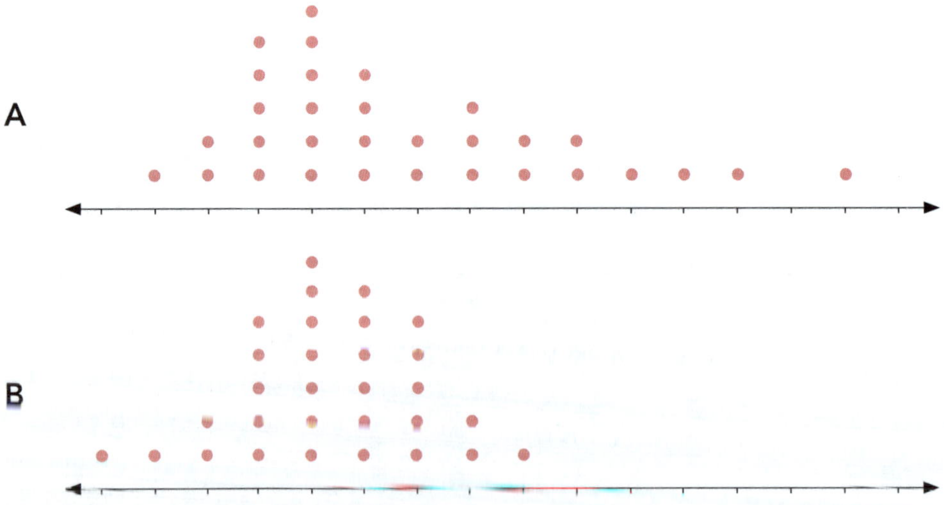

Spread: Distribution ______ is more spread than distribution ______.

Shape: Distribution A is ____,

and distribution B is ______.

 ISBN: 9780170447294

Scatter plots

- A scatter plot is used to show the **relationship** between **two variables**.
- These variables can be **continuous** or **discrete**.
- Each dot represents two pieces of data about one object, e.g. the height and mass of a person.
- Scatter plots are used to show data obtained from **relationship questions**.

Coordinates revision

- A positive **x** coordinate tells you how far to move to the **right**.
- A positive **y** coordinate tells you how far to move **up**.
- Coordinates are written in brackets, in alphabetical order: **(*x*, *y*)**.

Understanding scatter plots

Examples:

1

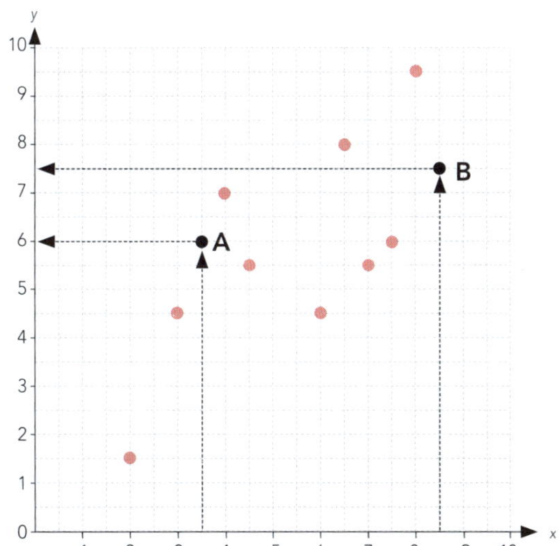

A (3.5, 6)

B (8.5, 7.5)

2 Some professional basketballers' heights and annual salaries are plotted on this graph.

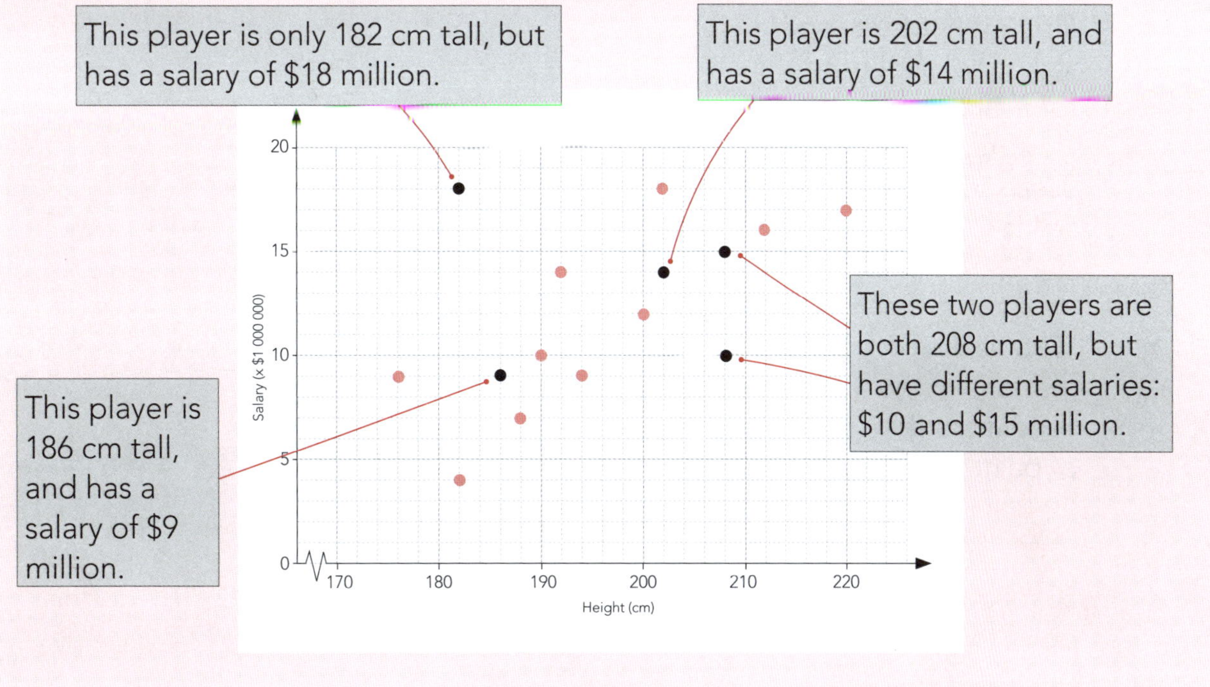

ISBN: 9780170447294

3 Scatter graphs can also be interpreted without numbers.

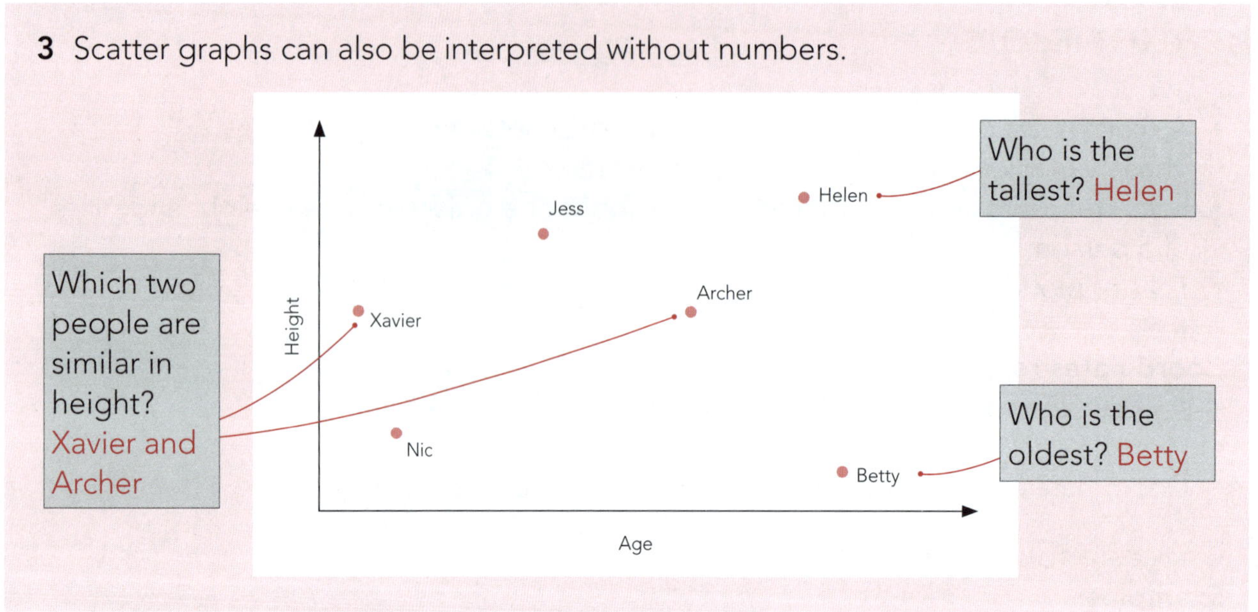

1 An artist recorded the amount of paint on an artwork and how much it sold for. Give the coordinates and description of:

Artist	Coordinates	Description
a	(______, ______)	They used ______ ml of paint and sold it for $________.
b	(______, ______)	They used ______ ml of paint and sold it for $________.

c 40 ml of paint was used on one artwork. How much did it sell for?

____

d One piece of art used very little paint but sold for a large amount. How much paint was used, and what did it sell for?

____

e What is the probability that one of the artworks used more than 60 ml of paint?

____

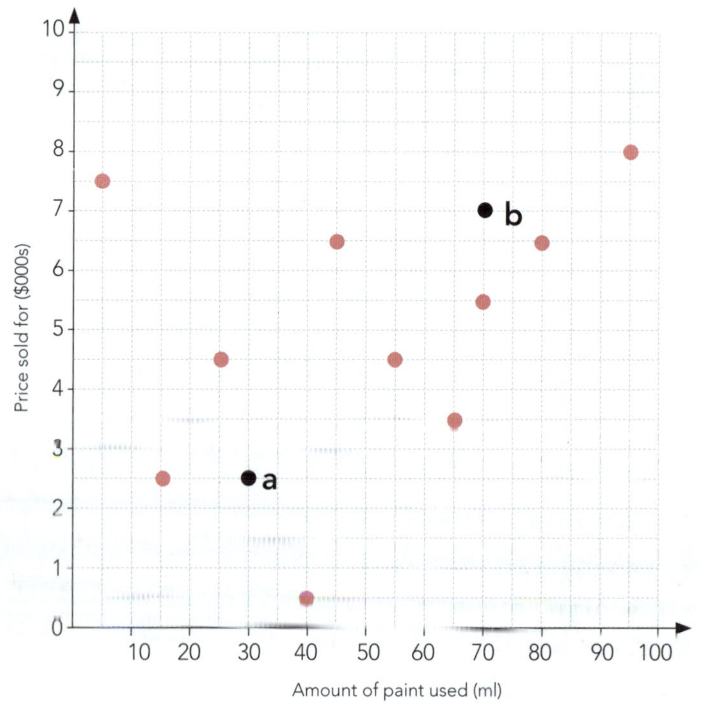

f 60 ml of paint was used on the latest artwork and it sold for $8500. Add this point to the graph.

ISBN: 9780170447294

2 Time spent studying and grades received were recorded.

Are these statements true or false?

a Douglas's grade was higher than Gabby's. True/False

b George spent the most time studying. True/False

c Mirabel spent more time studying, but got a lower grade than Henrietta. True/False

3 Music students were tracked to see if practice helped to reduce mistakes. Complete the table for students **a** and **b**.

Student	Coordinates	Description
a	(______, ______)	They practised for ____ hours and made _____ mistakes.
b	(______, ______)	They practised for ____ hours and made _____ mistakes.

Highlight and label the points for a student who:

c Practised for five and a half hours and made four mistakes (label 'c').

d Made seven mistakes and practised for one and a half hours (label 'd').

e What percentage of performers (including c and d) made fewer than four mistakes?

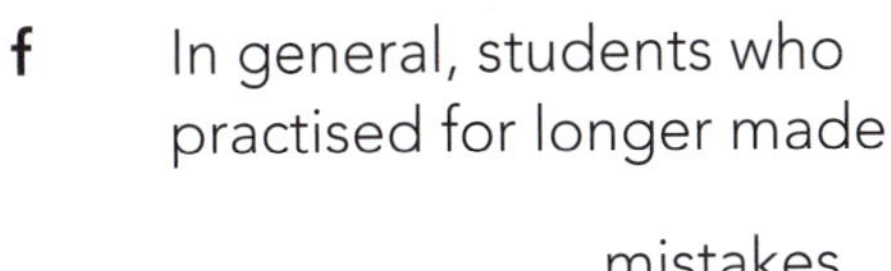

f In general, students who practised for longer made

______________ mistakes.

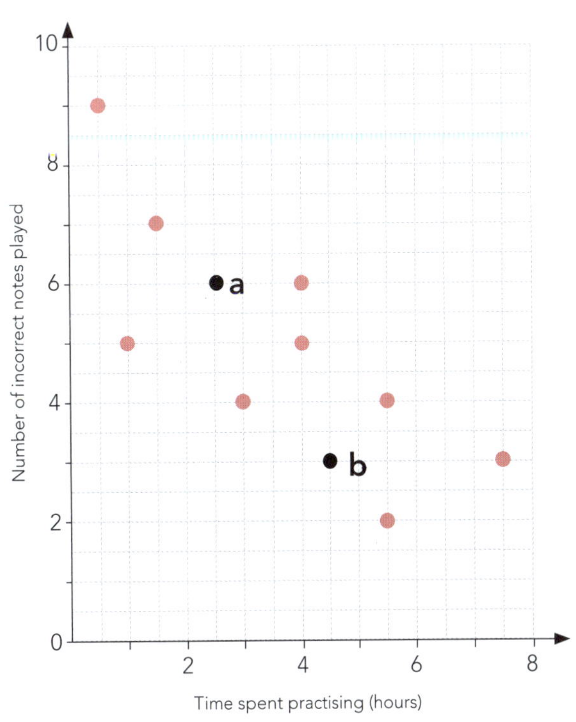

ISBN: 9780170447294

Describing and comparing features of scatter plots

Direction

Positive:

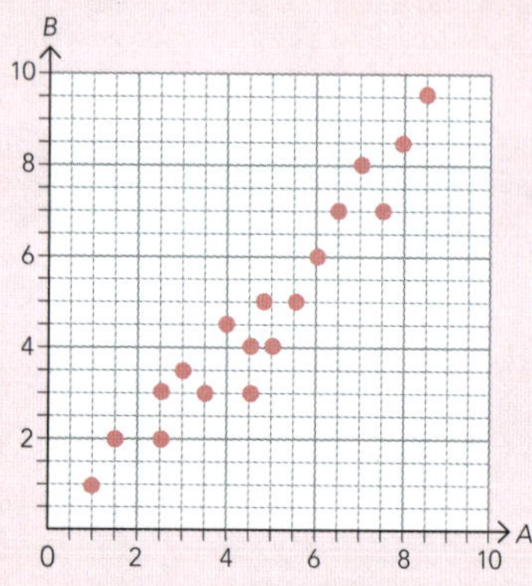

As *A* gets bigger, *B* gets **bigger**.

Negative:

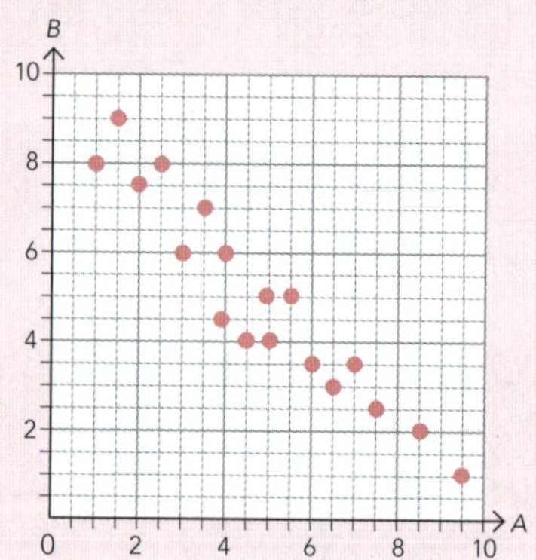

As *A* gets bigger, *B* gets **smaller**.

Strength

Strong:

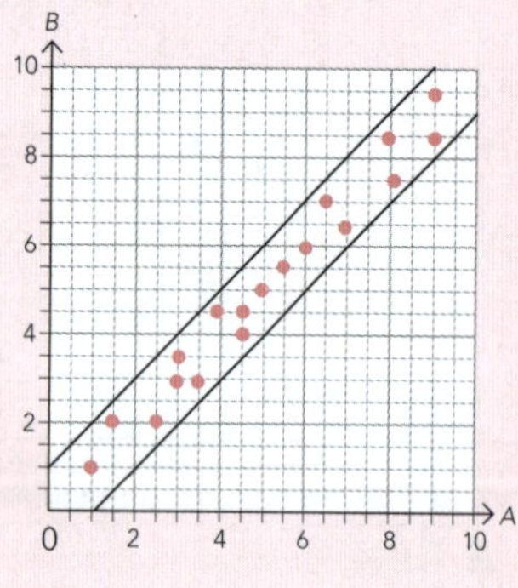

This means:

- You can have confidence that the relationship is strong.

Moderate:

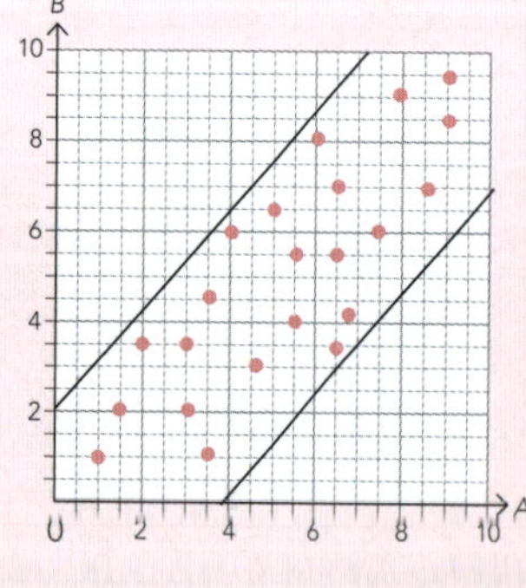

This means:

- The relationship is moderately strong.

Weak:

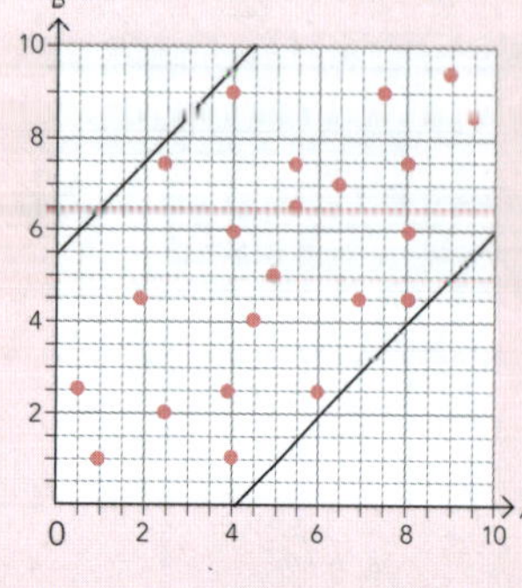

This means:

- The relationship is weak.

 ISBN: 9780170447294

Highlight the appropriate descriptors for these graphs.

4

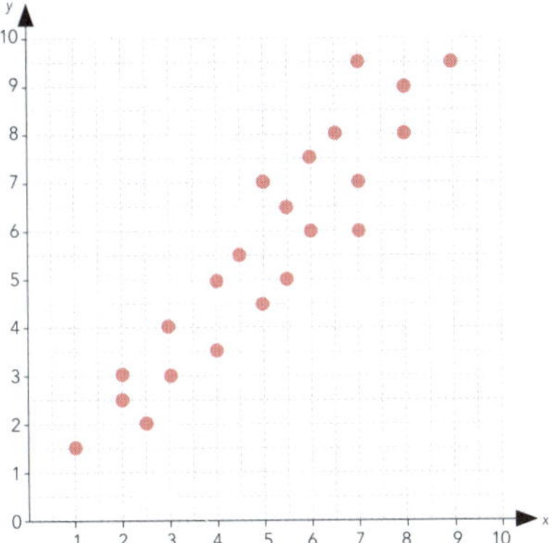

Direction: Positive/negative
Strength: Strong/moderate/weak

5

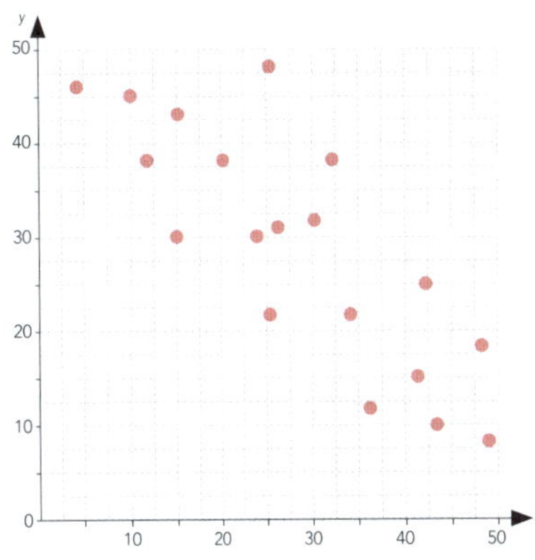

Direction: Positive/negative
Strength: Strong/moderate/weak

6

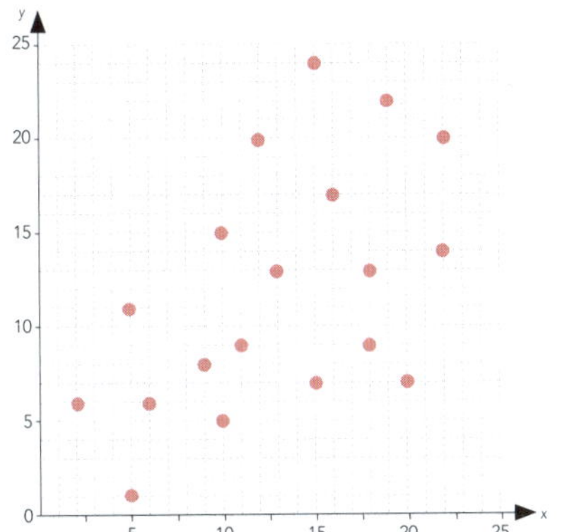

Direction: Positive/negative
Strength: Strong/moderate/weak

7

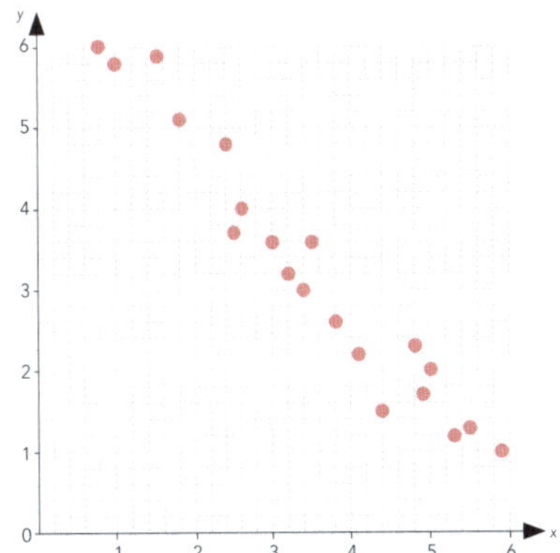

Direction: Positive/negative
Strength: Strong/moderate/weak

8 The graph shows the relationship between the length of a footprint and the height of the person who made it.

Footprint and height

Footprint (cm)

Height (cm)

The graph shows a ____________________ relationship between a person's height and the length of their footprint. This means that taller people have ____________________ footprints.

Data analysis

- There are three things that we need to know in order to be able to discuss and compare distributions:

  1 Where is the **centre** of the data?
  2 How widely is the data **spread**?
  3 Are there any unusual features?

Measures of centre (averages)

- There are **three** measures for the centre of data.

Name	Calculation	Advantages	Disadvantages
Mean	$\frac{\text{the sum of all the data values}}{\text{the number of data values}}$	• Easy to calculate	• Distorted by very big or small values
Median	middle value	• Usually a good measure of centre	• Data must be put in order
Mode	value that occurs most frequently	• Very easy to find	• Very unreliable as measure of centre • Often there are two or none

Mean

- The mean is sometimes falsely called the average.
- The numbers do not need to be in order for this calculation.
- Means are not always whole numbers, so sensible rounding may be needed.
- The mean is influenced by unusually large or small values.

$$\textbf{mean} = \frac{\textbf{sum of all the data values}}{\textbf{number of data values}}$$

Notice that 0 must be included in the calculation.

Example:

0 2 6 1 7 6 9 9 55

$$\text{Mean} = \frac{0+2+6+1+7+6+9+9+55}{9}$$
$$= 10.\dot{5}$$

There are 9 numbers in the data set.

The mean of this data set is $10.\dot{5}$ or 10.6 (1 dp).

Notice what happens to the mean if the 55 is removed.

0 2 6 1 7 6 9 9

$$\text{Mean} = \frac{0+2+6+1+7+6+9+9}{8}$$
$$= 5$$

There are now 8 numbers in the data set.

The mean of this data set is 5.

The 55 was so much larger than the other values that it influenced the mean.

 ISBN: 9780170447294

For these data sets, estimate the mean, and then calculate it.

1 **a** **4 31 32 35 38 39**

Estimate = ______ Mean = $\frac{4 + \qquad}{6}$

= ______

b **31 32 35 38 39**

Estimate = ______ Mean = ______________________

= ______

c The mean for set **b** is bigger/smaller than that for set **a** because ______________

____

Median

- If there is an **odd number of values** in a data, the median is the **middle number**.
- If there is an **even number of values**, the median is **halfway between the two middle numbers** in the data set.
- Before you can calculate the median, you must **put the data in order**.

Examples:

1 A data set with an odd number of values

15 22 13 34 14 26 18 29 19

Cross them off as you go, to make sure you don't miss any. Then check you have the same number of pieces of data.

Put them **in order** before finding the median: **13 14 15 18 19 22 26 29 34**

This is the middle number.

The median of this data set = 19.

2 A data set with an even number of values

41 42 45 45 48 59 59 90

These are the middle numbers. Add them together and divide by 2.

The median for this data set = $\frac{45 + 48}{2}$ = 46.5.

Notice that the median is not influenced by the unusually large value (90).

ISBN: 9780170447294

2 For these data sets, estimate the median, and then calculate it.

a **1 2 4 5 6 8 9 11 18 25 30 31**

Estimate = ____________ Median = ____________

b **7 9 12 13 15 21 22 24 27 29 31 35**

Estimate = ____________ Median = ____________

3 Find the medians of the following data sets.

a

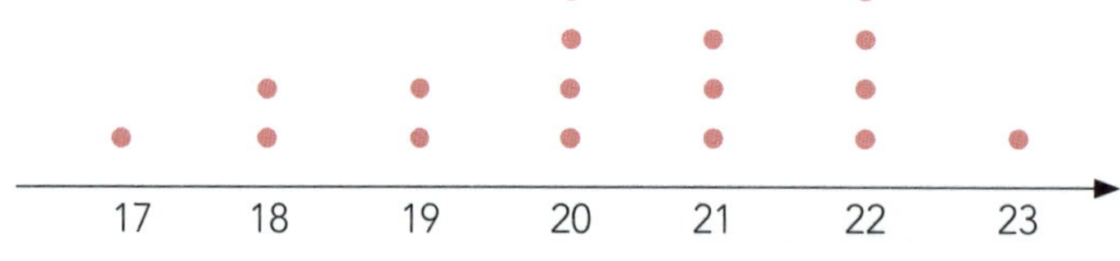

Median = ______

b

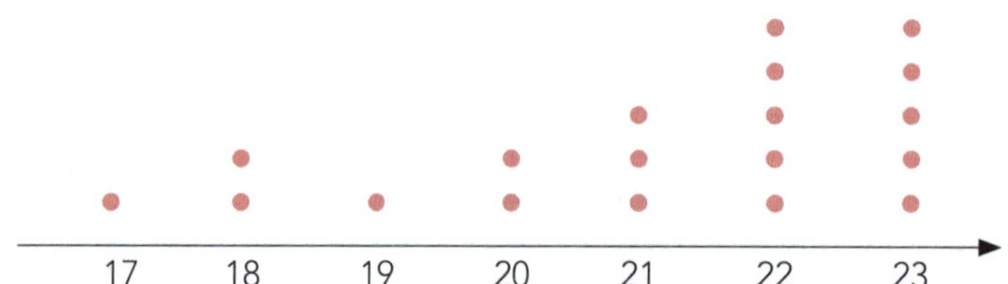

Median = ______

Mode

- The mode is the **most common value**.
- Sometimes there are **several modes**.
- If there are **three or more** numbers that occur equally often, we say there is **no mode**.

Examples:

1  **7 11 23**  **7 5**  **7 13 22 14 16 9 17 5**

The most common number is **7**: there are three of them.

The mode of this data set is 7.

2  **15 2 15 4 5 17 8 13 11 13 9 12 6**

Both **13** and **15** occur twice.

The modes are 13 and 15.

3 **46** 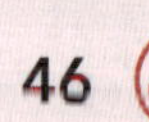 **45 52 39**  **45 47 49 52 41 44 49**

There are three numbers that occur equally often: **45**, **49** and **52**.

There is no mode.

If there are **three or more** 'modes', we say there is **no mode** at all.

 ISBN: 9780170447294

4 Find the mode(s) of these data sets.

a **24 33 19 26 28 14 17 18 25 14** Mode(s) = ____________

b **18 17 15 16 19 14 19 17 13 20** Mode(s) = ____________

c **51 61 53 64 51 64 61 69 53 54** Mode(s) = ____________

5 Calculate the mean, median and mode for these data sets.

a

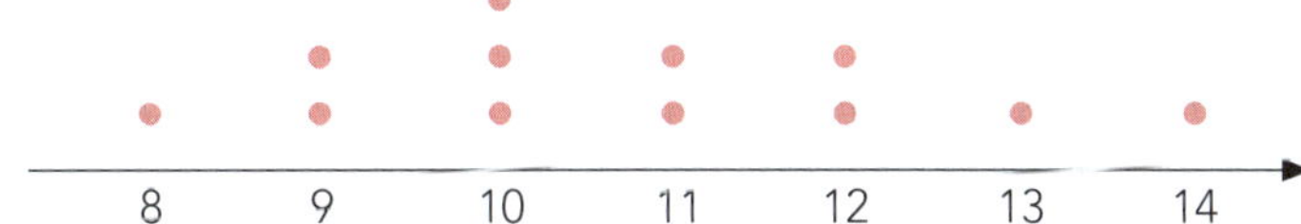

Mean = ________ Median = ________ Mode = ________

b

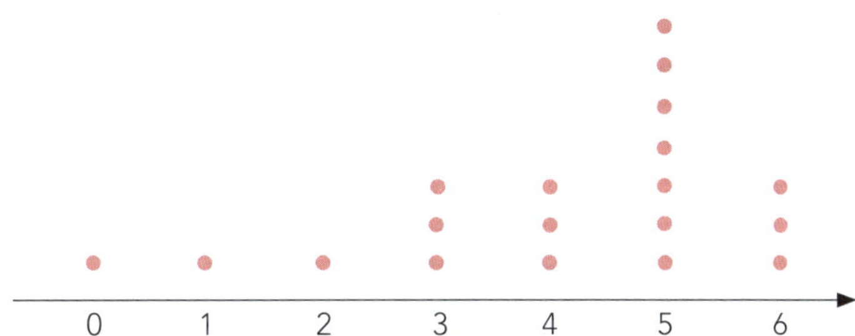

Mean = ________ Median = ________ Mode = ________

Why is the mean smaller than the median and the mode?

____

c

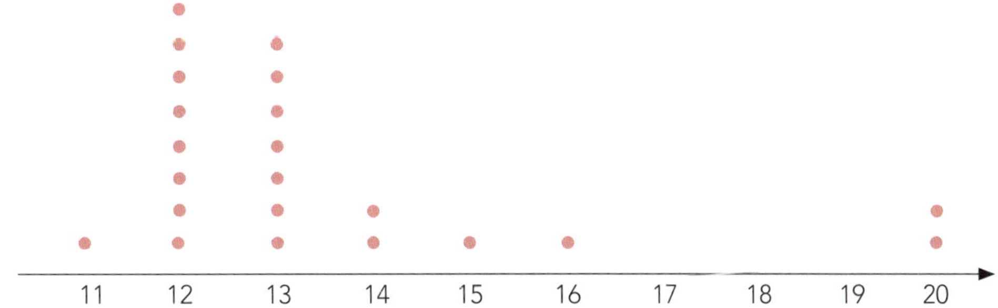

Mean = ________ Median = ________ Mode = ________

Why is the mean bigger than the median and the mode?

____

ISBN: 9780170447294

Measures of spread

Range

- The range is the **maximum value minus the minimum value** in the data set.
- Note: the range is a **single number**.
- Like the mean, the range is affected by unusually large or small values.
- The data does not need to be in order to calculate the range.
- The range is a measure of the **variability** of the data.

Range = maximum – minimum

Quartiles

- The upper quartile (UQ) is the **median** of the **top half** of the data.
- The lower quartile (LQ) is the **median** of the **bottom half** of the data.
- The quartiles and the median divide the data into **quarters**.

Interquartile range (IQR) = upper quartile (UQ) – lower quartile (LQ)

Examples:

1 If the number of pieces of data is **odd**, **exclude** the median from the top and bottom halves of the data.

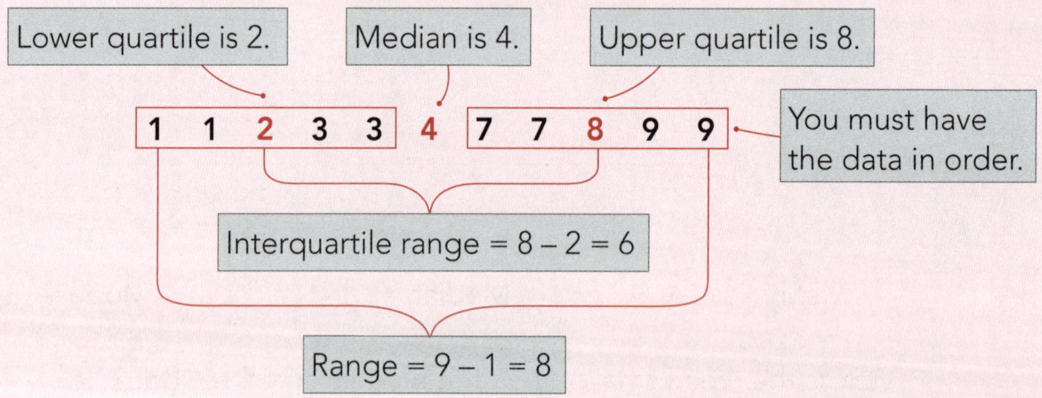

2 If the number of pieces of data is **even**, find the median of the top and bottom halves of the data.

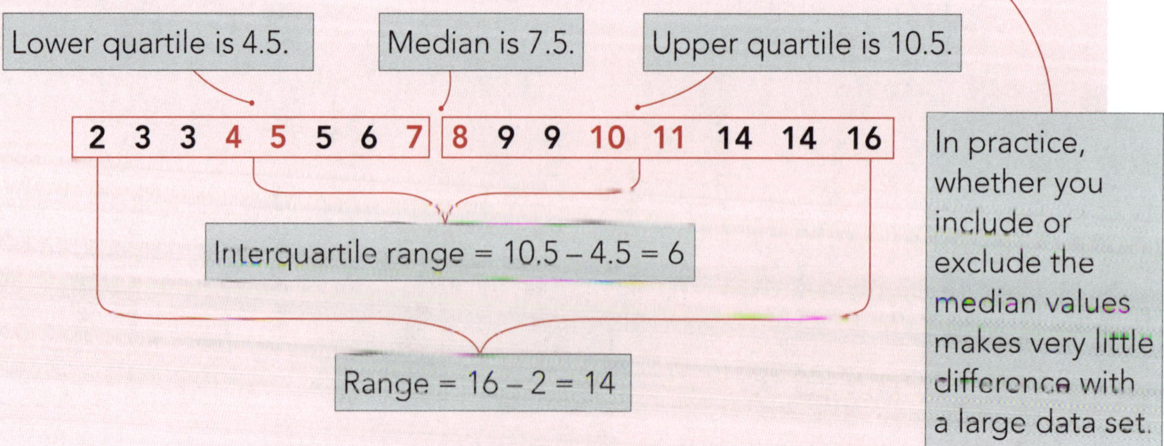

Ranges and interquartile ranges are used to measure the variability of groups of data.

ISBN: 9780170447294

Calculate the statistics for the following data sets.

1 **1 3 5 8 9 10 11 11 15 17 18**

Minimum = _____ LQ = _____ Median = _____ UQ = _____ Maximum = _____

Range = _______________ Interquartile range = _______________

2 **0 2 2 4 6 7 8 9 9 10 11 18 20 21**

Minimum = _____ LQ = _____ Median = _____ UQ = _____ Maximum = _____

Range = _______________ Interquartile range = _______________

Put the data in order, then calculate the statistics for these data sets.

3 **2 2 3 3 4 5 5 7 7 7 9 9 10 14 16**

Minimum = _____ LQ = _____ Median = _____ UQ = _____ Maximum = _____

Range = _______________ Interquartile range = _______________

4 **7 9 12 12 14 16 16 18 19 19 20 21 24**

Minimum = _____ LQ = _____ Median = _____ UQ = _____ Maximum =

Range = _______________ Interquartile range = _______________

5 **19 45 53 57 78 82 83 89 96 104 105 106**

Minimum = _____ LQ = _____ Median = _____ UQ = _____ Maximum = _____

Range = _______________ Interquartile range = _______________

ISBN: 9780170447294

6 **1.2 1.3 1.3 1.4 1.4 1.4 1.5 1.6 1.8 1.9 1.9**

Minimum = _____ LQ = _____ Median = _____ UQ = _____ Maximum = _____

Range = _______________ Interquartile range = _______________

7

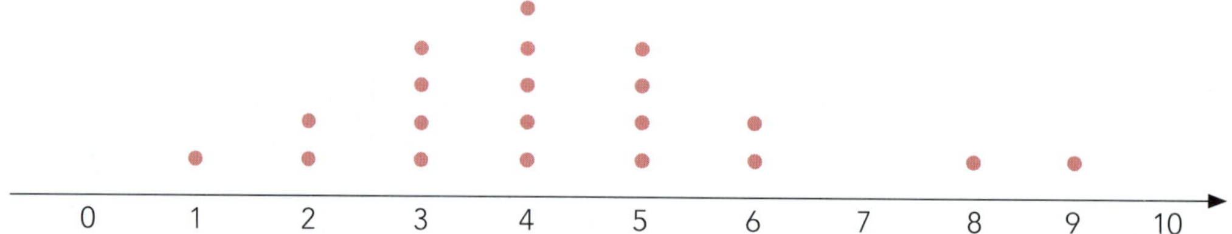

Minimum = _____ LQ = _____ Median = _____ UQ = _____ Maximum = _____

Range = _______________ Interquartile range = _______________

8

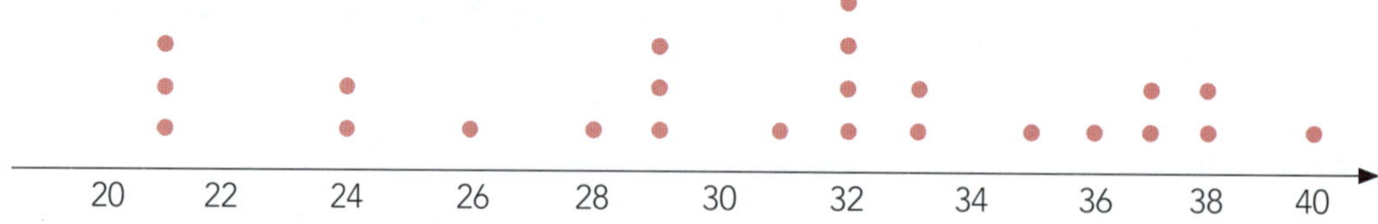

Minimum = _____ LQ = _____ Median = _____ UQ = _____ Maximum = _____

Range = _______________ Interquartile range = _______________

9

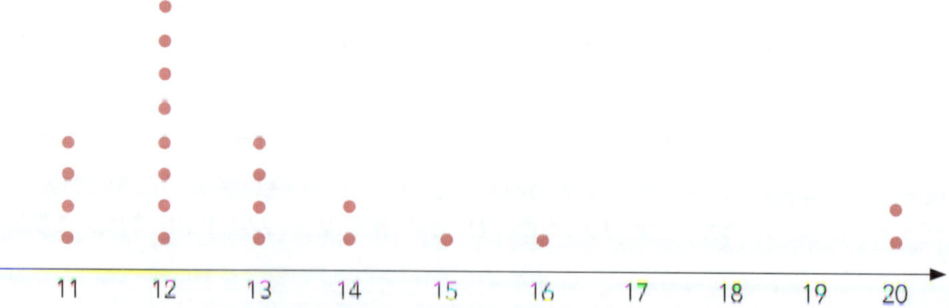

Minimum = _____ LQ = _____ Median = _____ UQ = _____ Maximum = _____

Range = _______________ Interquartile range = _______________

ISBN: 9780170447294

Unusual features

- These could be an **unusual point** or **clusters**.
- An unusual point is one that is away from the rest of the data.
- A cluster is a group of data that is away from the rest of the data.

How many makes a cluster?
Don't get hung up on labels and definitions. It's best to write what you see. If there are two points away from the rest, then say that!

Examples:

1 An unusual point

Arm spans of Year 10 students in cm: **161 149 158 175 160 203 151 156**

This student's arm span is unusual because it's 28 cm larger than the next longest arm span.

2 It is often easiest to see unusual points and clusters when the data is graphed.

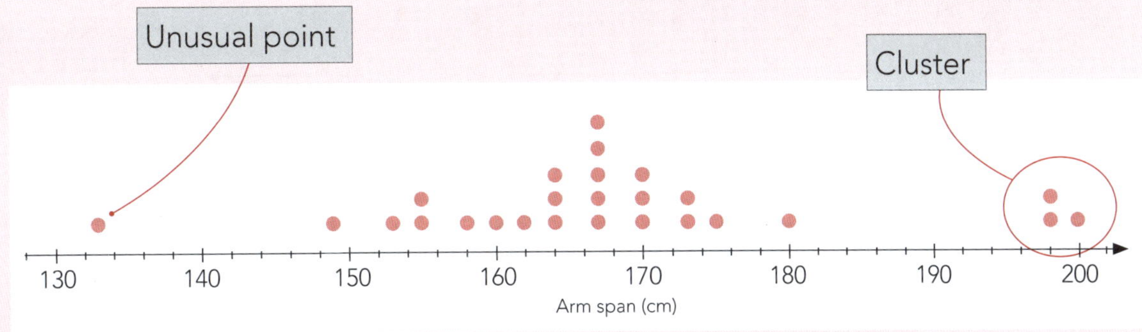

Note: **1** Check that unusual points are not mistakes in measurement, counting or recording.

2 Include them when you graph and analyse your data. Think about whether the unusual feature is possible and state your thoughts when you discuss the data.

Circle or highlight any unusual features in these data sets and state whether they are clusters or unusual points.

1

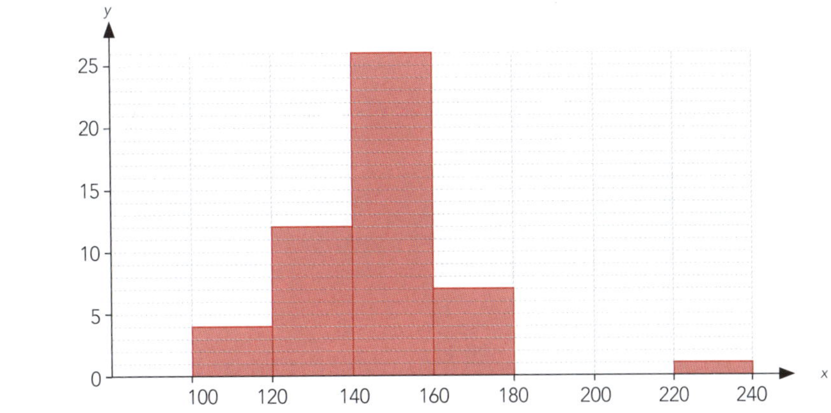

ISBN: 9780170447294

2

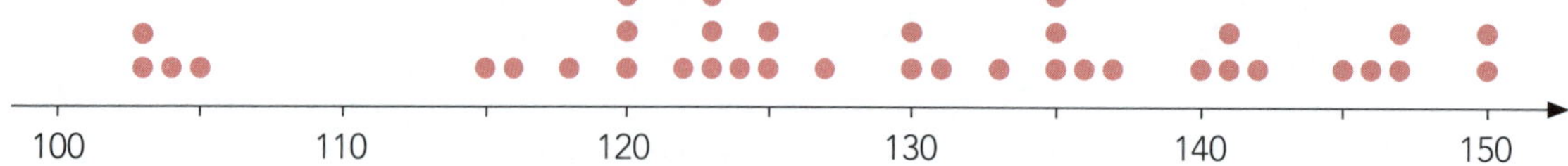

3

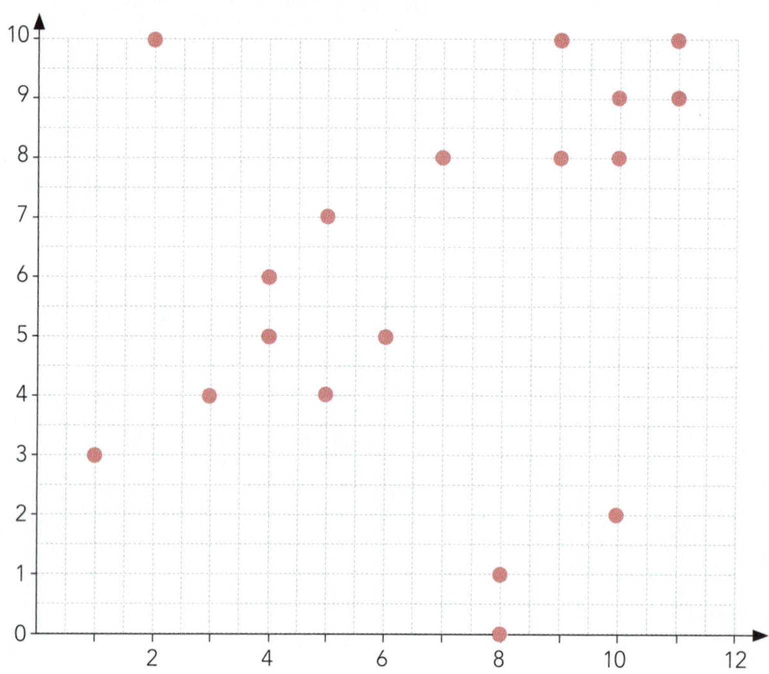

4 **35 29 25 27 13 29 32 51 32 34**

5

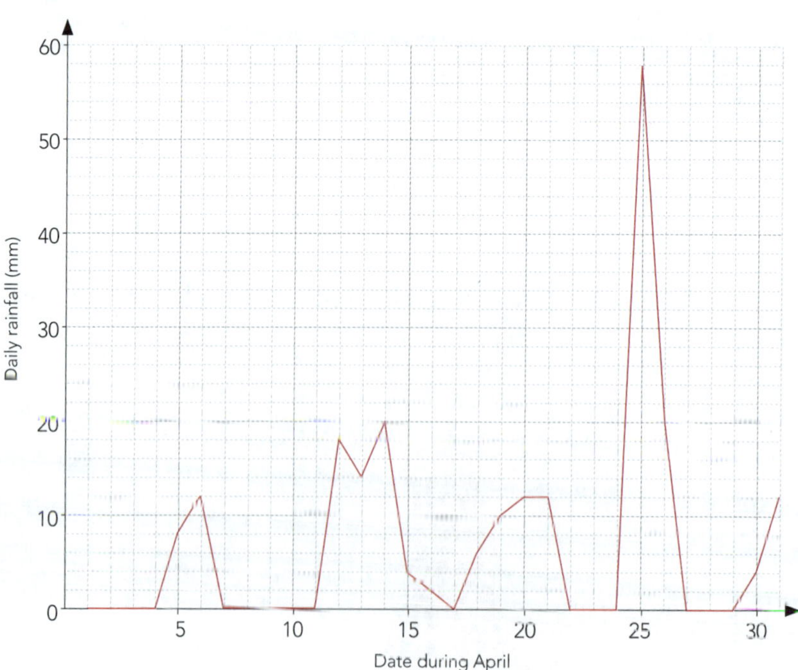

What makes the point unusual? ______________________________

____

 ISBN: 9780170447294

Effects of unusual points

- The **mean** and the **range** are **affected** by unusual points.
- The **median**, **mode**, **quartiles** and **interquartile range** are **usually unaffected**.
- The mean is the only average that uses **every** piece of data.

No unusual points ⇒ either the **median or mean** are usually good measures of centre.

Unusual points ⇒ likely that the **median** is a better measure of centre, and the **IQR** is likely to be the best measure of spread.

Examples:

1 **4 5 5 6 7 8 25**

Mean $= \frac{60}{7}$ $= 8.57$ (2 dp)

Median = 6

Range = 25 – 4 = 21

IQR = 8 – 5 = 3

The median (6) is a better measure of centre than the mean (8.57) because the mean is larger than all but one value in the data set.

The IQR (3) is a better measure of spread than the range (21) because the range of the lowest six numbers is only 4.

2 A chef asked people to rate her food out of 10. These were the results:

1 1 1 6 6 6 7 8 8

Median = 6

Mean $= \frac{1+1+1+6+6+6+7+8+8}{9}$ $= 4.\dot{8}$

Median ⇒ most people were happy with her food.

Mean ⇒ most people were not happy with her food.

In this situation, because most people scored her food at 6 or more, it would be more appropriate to use the median as the measure of centre.

Calculate the median and the mean for these data sets and name the best measure of centre if there is one.

6 **3 5 6 8 9 9 12 36**

Median = ________ Mean = ________

Best measure(s) of centre: ____________________, because ____________

____

ISBN: 9780170447294

7 **12 15 16 18 18 19 21 24 25**

Median = ________ Mean = ________

Best measure(s) of centre: ____________________________, because ______________

____

8 **2 34 57 63 72 74 76 81 88 89**

Median = ________ Mean = ________

Best measure(s) of centre: ____________________________, because ______________

____

9

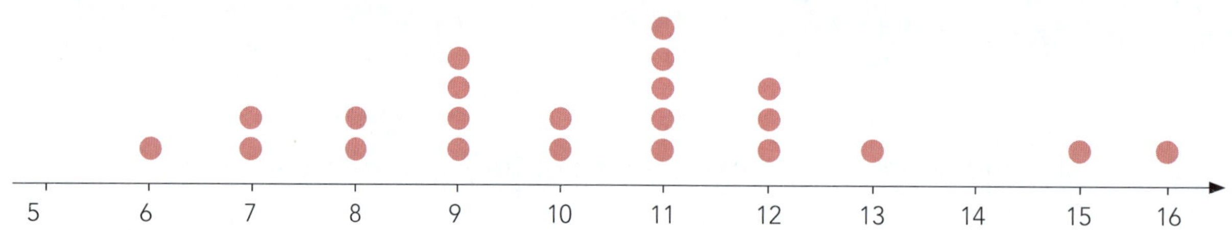

Median = ________ Mean = ________

Best measure(s) of centre: ____________________________, because ______________

____

10

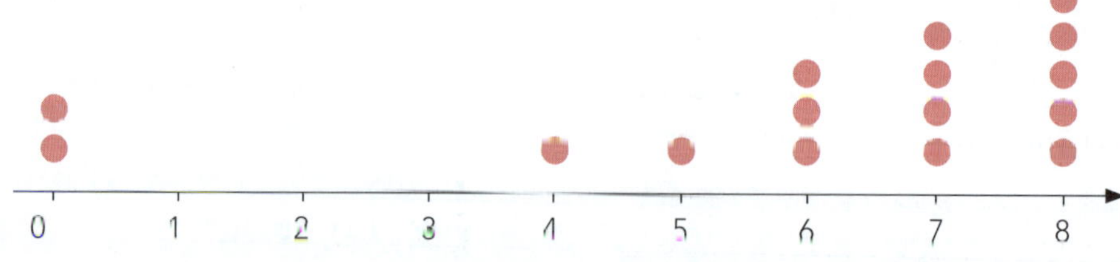

Median = ________ Mean = ________

Best measure(s) of centre: ____________________________, because ______________

____

ISBN: 9780170447294

Challenge 2

1 The following data sets are in ascending order. Find the missing numbers.

a **2 3 6 10 11 17 ☐** — has a range of 15.

b **2 2 3 ☐ 8 8 9 10** — has mode of 8 and a median of 7.5.

c **3 5 6 8 ☐ 13 18 19 19 19** — has a median of 11.

d **4 7 ☐ 9 9 12 15** — has a mean of 9.

e **4 5 7 7 ☐ ☐** — has a mean of 7 and a range of 6.

f **☐ 9 11 11 13 ☐ 18** — has an interquartile range of 8 and a mean of 12.

2 The following data sets are not in order. Find the missing numbers.

a **☐ 18 14 7 15 19** — has a mean of 13.

b **☐ 10 2 16 7** — has a median of 10.

c **☐ 20 4 8 20 12** — has a mean of 12.

3 Here are two data sets. Find the missing numbers.

Set A	8	3	6
Set B	7		
Set C	9		

Clues:

1 All three sets have the same mean.
2 Set A has the same median as set B.
3 Set C has double the range of set B.

Box plots

- These are used to display **discrete** or **continuous** data.
- They are very useful for comparing sets of data.
- These are sometimes called '**box and whisker plots**'. The whiskers are the lines between the box and the highest and lowest values.

Positions of the minimum, lower quartile, median, upper quartile and maximum

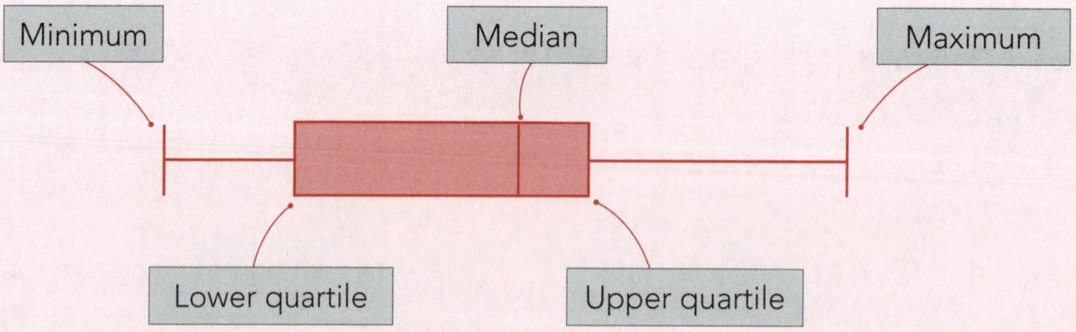

Minimum

Median

Maximum

Lower quartile

Upper quartile

Example:

1 3 4 5 6 6 8 9 9 10 11 11 12 14

Minimum 1 | LQ 5 | Median 8.5 | UQ 11 | Maximum 14

These 5 points divide the data into quarters.

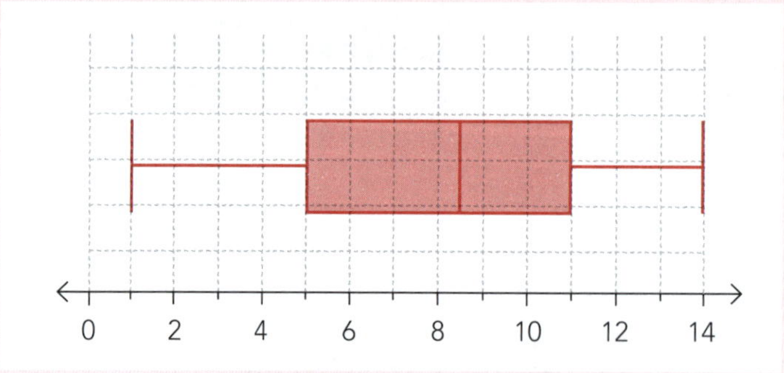

0 2 4 6 8 10 12 14

Draw a box plot for these statistics.

1 Minimum = 4 LQ = 6 Median = 11 UQ = 14 Maximum = 19

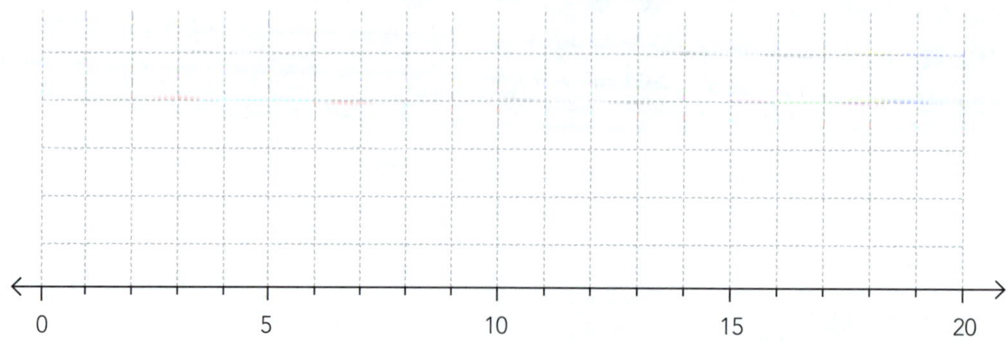

 ISBN: 9780170447294

Calculate the required statistics and then draw box plots for the following.

2 **2 2 4 5 6 6 7 9 10 14 16 18 19 19**

Minimum = ____ LQ = ____ Median = ____ UQ = ____ Maximum = ____

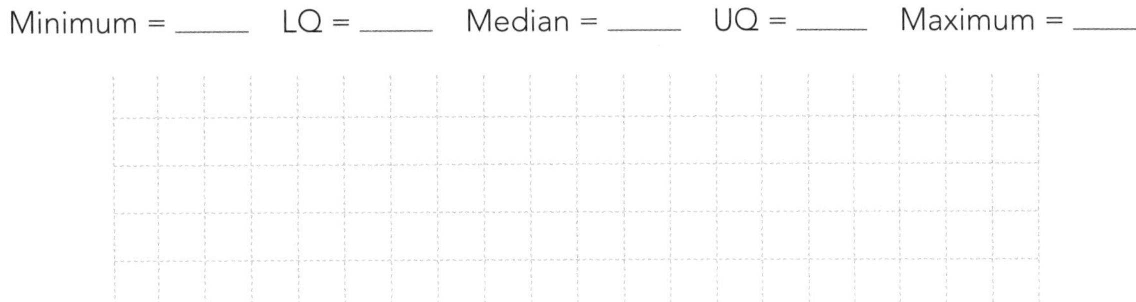

3 **0 3 4 4 5 7 9 9 10 12 14 14 15 18 19 20 20**

Minimum = ____ LQ = ____ Median = ____ UQ = ____ Maximum = ____

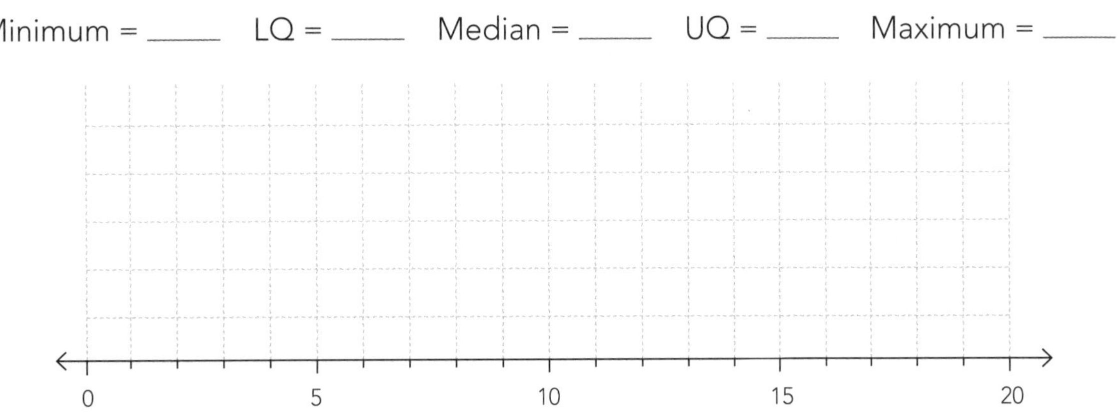

4 **0 1 3 3 5 5 7 8 9 12 14 17 19**

Minimum = ____ LQ = ____ Median = ____ UQ = ____ Maximum = ____

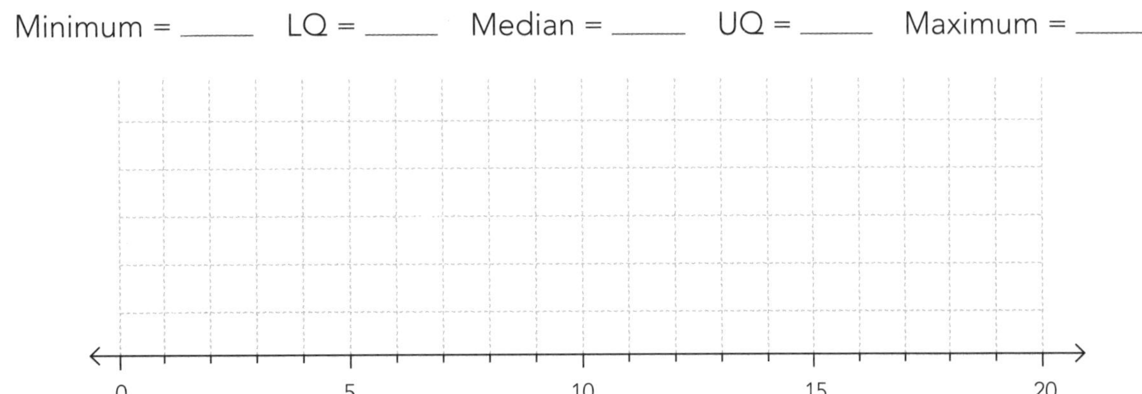

ISBN: 9780170447294

Understanding box plots

You need to understand the meanings of different parts of a box plot.

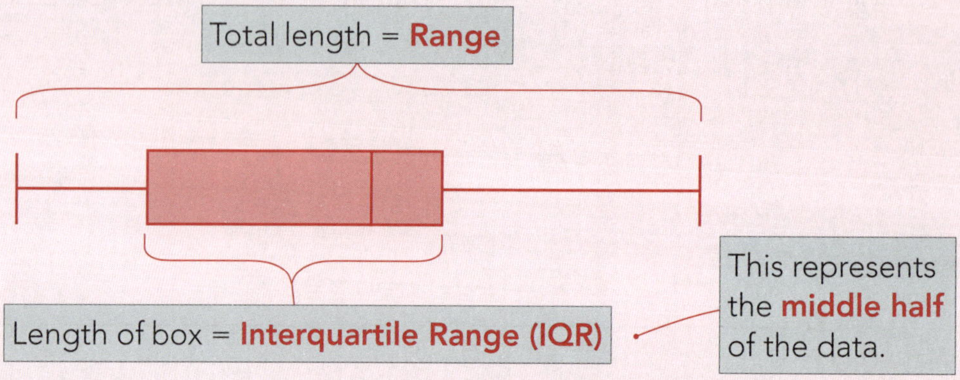

Total length = **Range**

Length of box = **Interquartile Range (IQR)**

This represents the **middle half** of the data.

Data is symmetrically distributed ⇒ box plot will be symmetrical.

Data is not symmetrically distributed ⇒ box plot will not be symmetrical.

Example:

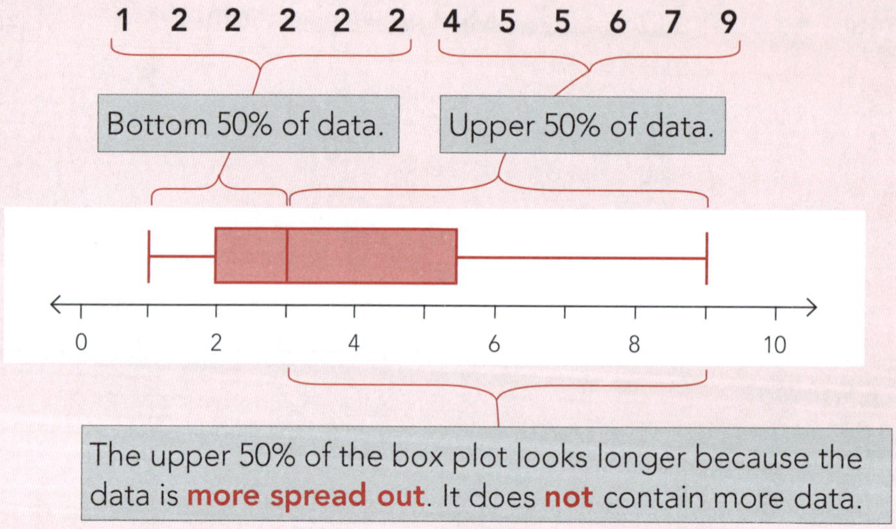

1 2 2 2 2 2 4 5 5 6 7 9

Bottom 50% of data.

Upper 50% of data.

0 2 4 6 8 10

The upper 50% of the box plot looks longer because the data is **more spread out**. It does **not** contain more data.

The **vertical lines** on a box plot divide the data into **quarters**.

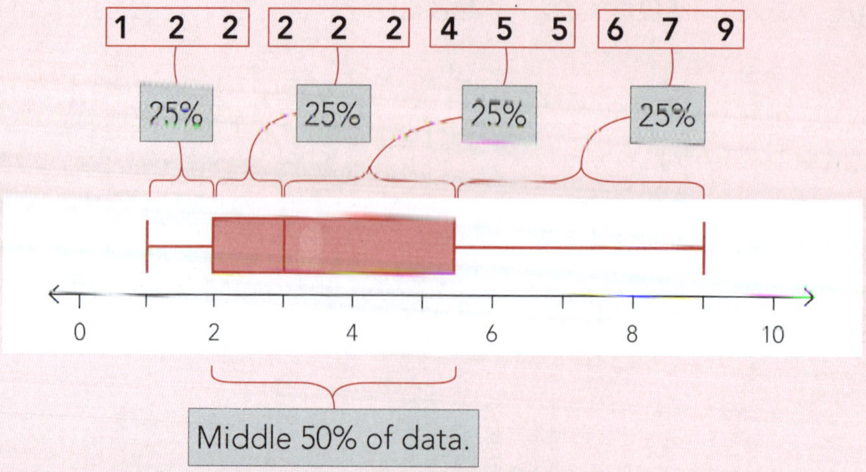

1 2 2 | 2 2 2 | 4 5 5 | 6 7 9

25% 25% 25% 25%

0 2 4 6 8 10

Middle 50% of data.

 ISBN: 9780170447294

Fill in the percentages missing from the boxes and the terms missing from the lines.

1

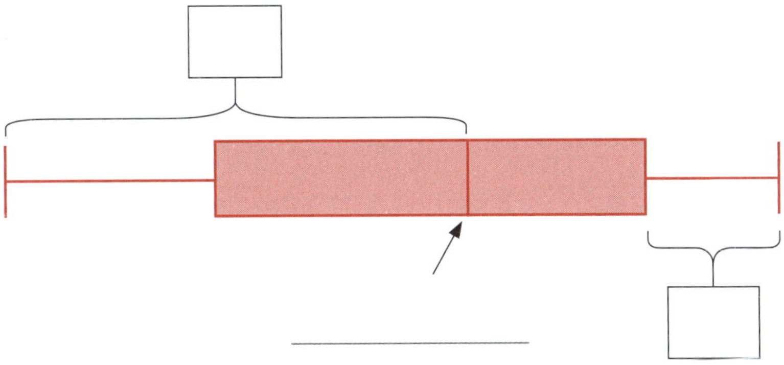

2

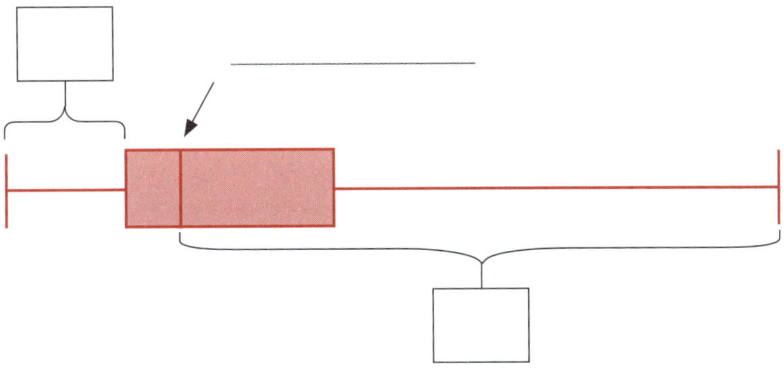

3

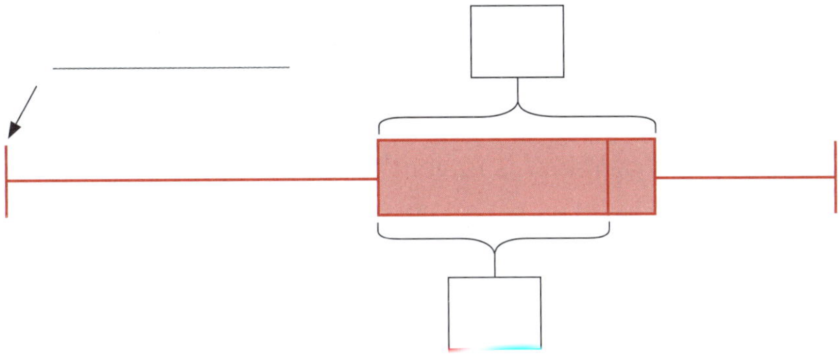

4

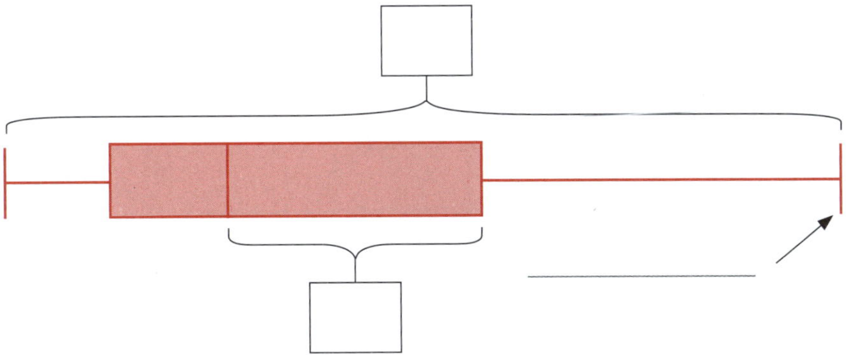

Comparing box plots

Box plots are a useful way of comparing several groups of data.

Example:

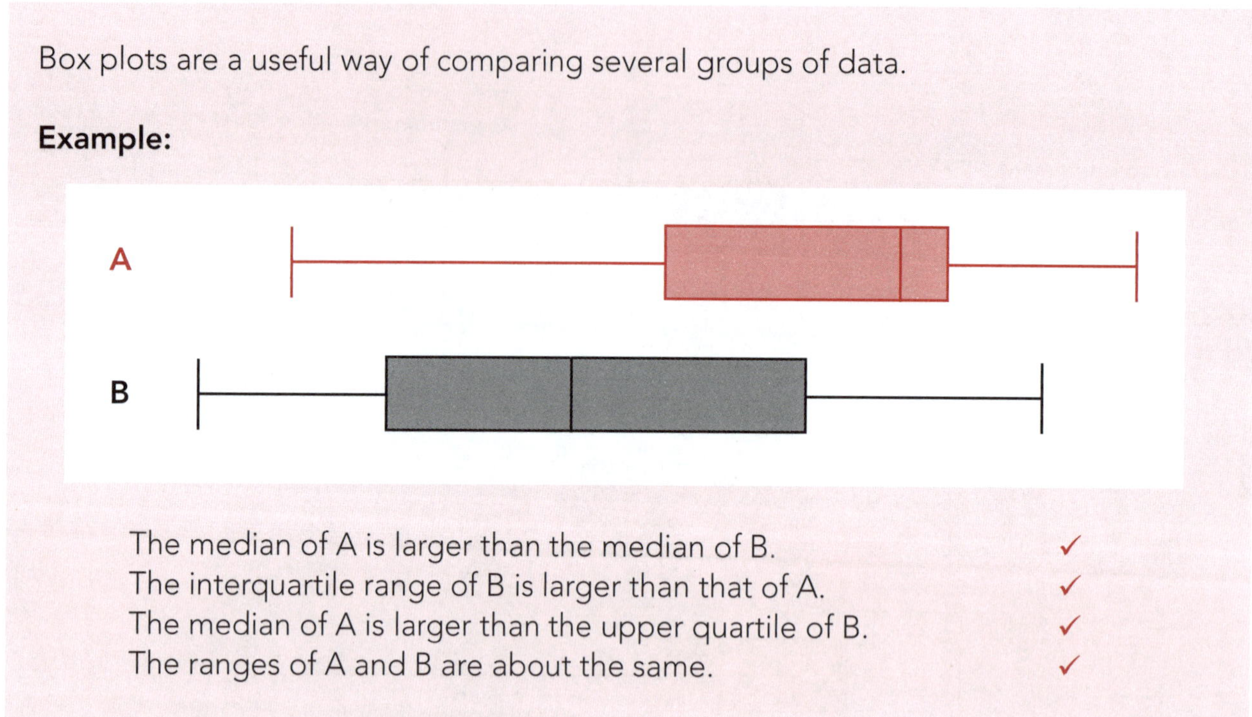

The median of A is larger than the median of B. ✓
The interquartile range of B is larger than that of A. ✓
The median of A is larger than the upper quartile of B. ✓
The ranges of A and B are about the same. ✓

Use ticks and crosses to show whether each statement is true or not.

1

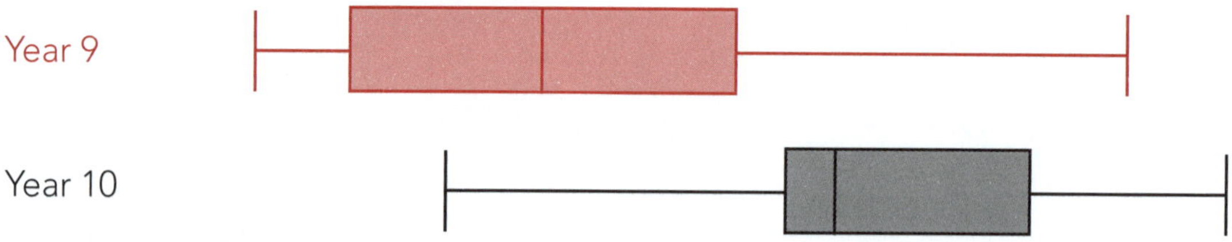

Year 9

Year 10

- **a** The maximum of Year 9 is lower than the maximum of Year 10. ☐
- **b** The median of Year 10 is higher than the upper quartile of Year 9. ☐
- **c** The lower quartile of Year 9 is higher than the minimum of Year 10. ☐

2

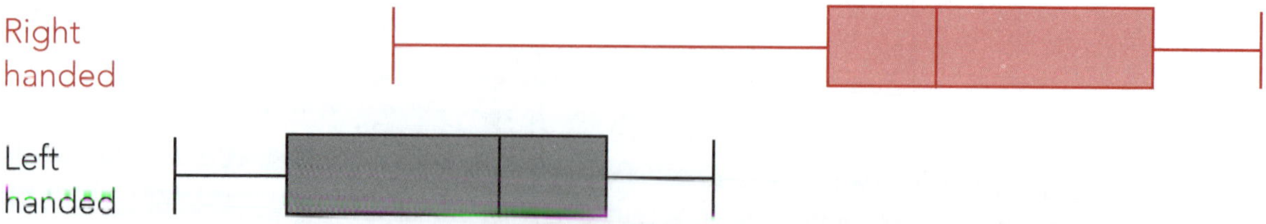

Right handed

Left handed

- **a** The minimum of right handed is higher than the upper quartile for left handed. ☐
- **b** The lower quartile of right handed is the same as the maximum for left handed. ☐
- **c** The median of right handed is larger than maximum for left handed. ☐

  ISBN: 9780170447294

Infographics

- Infographics are modifications of traditional graphs or diagrams used to convey numerical information.
- They are often visually pleasing, but they don't always make the message clearer.

Answer the following questions.

1 This infographic shows the heights (m) of ski fields in the South Island.

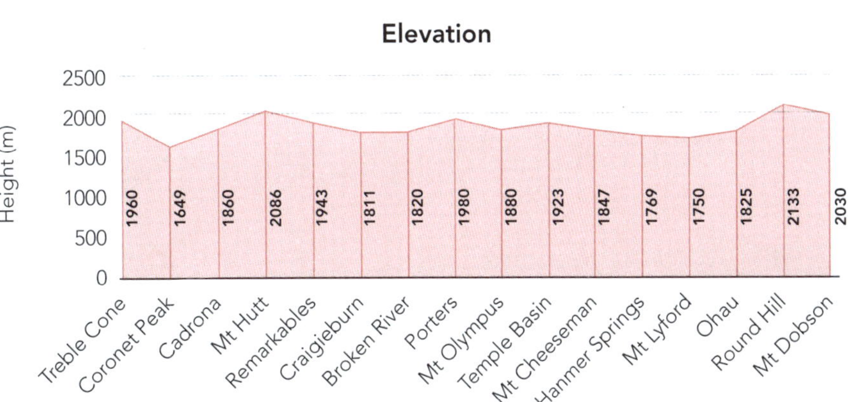

a What is the height of Mount Hutt ski field? __________

b What is the highest ski field in the South Island? __________

c What is the difference between the heights of the highest and lowest ski fields in the South Island? __________

2 This infographic shows the values of different types of non-alcoholic beverages sold globally during 2021.

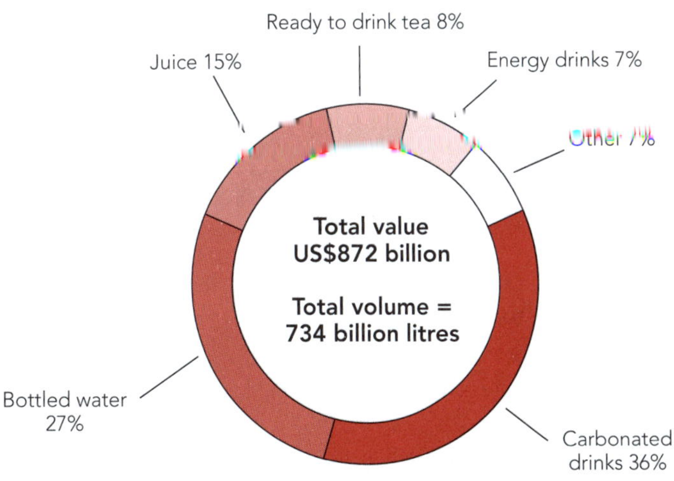

a What percentage of these was bottled water? __________

b Calculate the volume of energy drinks sold in 2021. __________

c What was the value of juice sold in 2021? __________

ISBN: 9780170447294

3 This infographic shows the percentage of people using each of these channels, sites and stations in New Zealand during 2020.

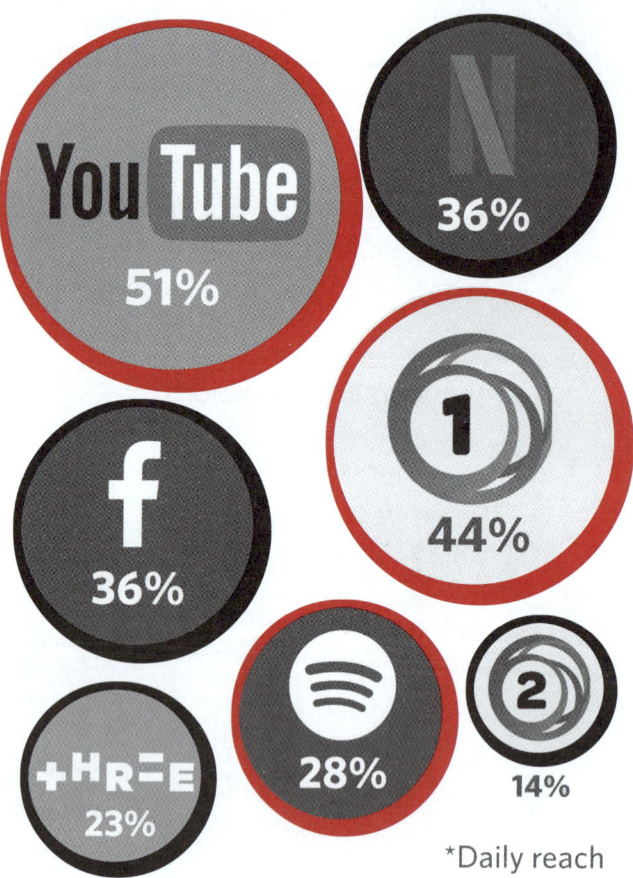

a Which was the least popular? ______________________

b Which was used by 23% of people? ______________________

c Which channels, sites or stations were used by more than 40% of people? ______________________

d Why do you think these percentages do not add to 100? ______________________

____

4 This infographic shows the most used and most trusted of the media as sources of news during Covid-19 lockdowns.

a What was the most used source? ______________________

b What percentage of people used the *New Zealand Herald*? ______________________

c What was the second most trusted source? ______________________

d Which had the biggest gap between trust and use? ______________________

e What percentage of people who used RNZ also trusted them? ______________________

 ISBN: 9780170447294

5 This infographic displays the percentage of New Zealand adults who have a post-school qualification in different fields of study.

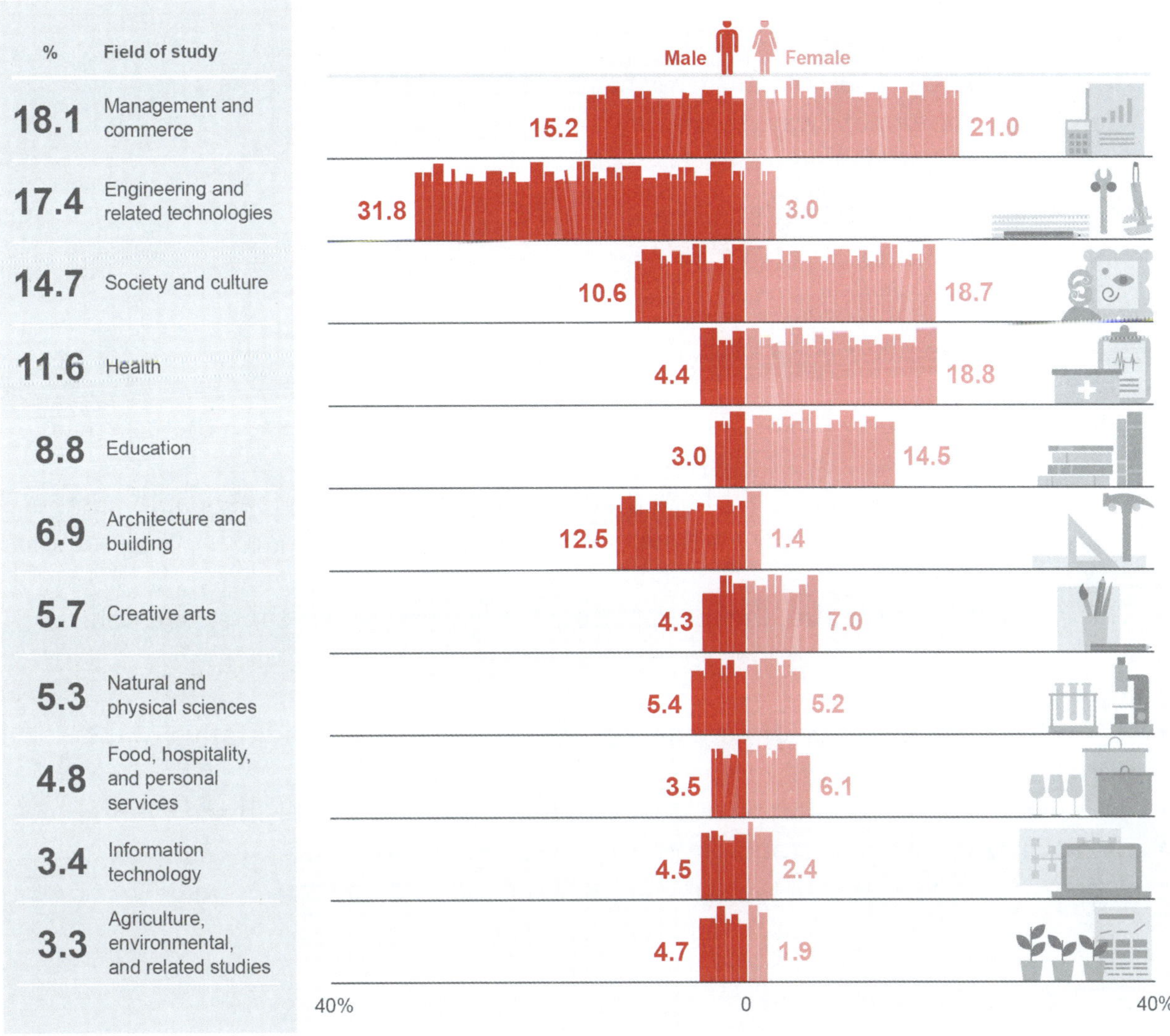

a What percentage study creative arts and are female? __________

b Which field of study has similar percentages of females and males?

____

c Which field of study has the biggest difference in genders?

____

d Around 745 000 adults are studying in New Zealand at any one time. How many of these would you expect to be:

i a male studying health? __________

ii a female studying education? __________

iii studying information technology? __________

ISBN: 9780170447294

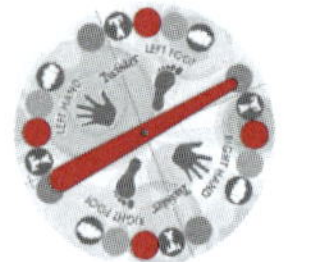

Statistical literacy

Statistical literacy is about:
- deciding whether a sample or survey has been done **fairly**
- identifying appropriate ways to display data **fairly**
- **being critical** about what you see or read
- **justifying** conclusions based on data and displays.

Sampling and bias

Sample size
- Each sample needs to be **large enough** to ensure that it reflects the characteristics of the population.
- As a loose guide, around 10% of the population is considered a reasonable number.
- However, time, cost and convenience need to be considered when deciding sample size.
- The larger the sample size, the more closely it is likely to reflect the population.

Sampling method
- It's important that the survey captures responses that are **representative** of the population.
- If a sample isn't representative of the population, then we say it is **biased (unfair)**.
- **Bias** occurs when some group or groups are not selected fairly.
- A **biased** sample **is not truly representative** of the population.

1 Complete the diagram below.

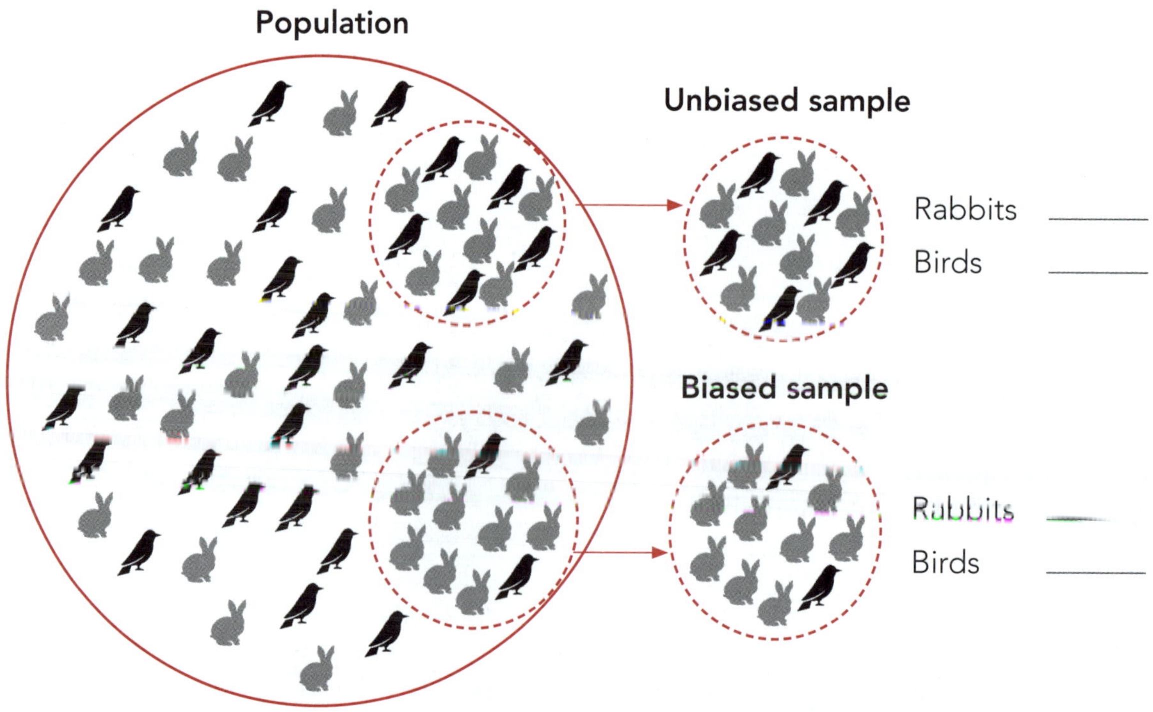

 ISBN: 9780170447294

For these situations, is the sample size big enough? Is the sample fair or biased?

	Situation	**Big enough sample?**	**Fair or biased?**
2	All students with surnames that started with 'Y' were surveyed about their thoughts on the school uniform.		
	Why?		
3	Members of the A netball team were surveyed about their thoughts on the school sports uniform.		
	Why?		
4	Every tenth student entering through the school gates was asked whether they thought sun hats should be allowed to be worn during lunchtimes.		
	Why?		
5	The first 50 students arriving at an assembly were asked what they thought the theme for the school social should be.		
	Why?		

Explain why these samples are likely to produce biased (unfair) results.

6 Customers at the drive-through of a fast food outlet were asked to name their favourite product.

____

7 People at the bowls club were asked for their opinions about a new shopping centre.

____

8 A radio station asked people to text or email who they thought would win a rugby test.

____

9 Drivers of utes passing through the testing station were asked whether they thought the service they received was satisfactory.

____

10 Members of the garden club were asked their opinions about cutting down trees in the local park.

____

ISBN: 9780170447294

Question types and appropriate data displays

Highlight the question and graph types that are appropriate for each question. There may be several suitable graphs.

	Question	Question type	Graph types
1	What percentage of girls and boys ate fast food at least once a week?	Summary Comparative Relationship	Pie graph Line graph Tally chart Bar graph
2	How long did you spend exercising each day during the last month?	Summary Comparative Relationship	Bar graph Line graph Scatter graph Histogram
3	What is your favourite dog breed?	Summary Comparative Relationship	Dot plot Bar graph Pie graph Tally chart
4	What is the relationship between the ages and weights of the lambs on Eru's farm?	Summary Comparative Relationship	Bar graph Line graph Scatter graph Histogram
5	How much time did members of the class spend on devices yesterday?	Summary Comparative Relationship	Tally chart Histogram Line graph Bar graph
6	How many absences were there each day during last term?	Summary Comparative Relationship	Strip graph Line graph Scatter plot Dot plot
7	What percentage of Year 9 and Year 10 students would like a junior formal?	Summary Comparative Relationship	Strip graph Dot plot Histogram Bar graph

 ISBN: 9780170447294

Data interpretation

- When interpreting graphs, you need to explain your reasoning.
- Sometimes there are several correct answers. This can lead to interesting discussion.
- Sometimes published graphs are misleading or incorrect.
- This may be intentional or careless. It pays to think carefully about the information and who presented it.

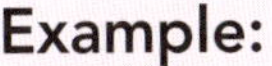
Example:

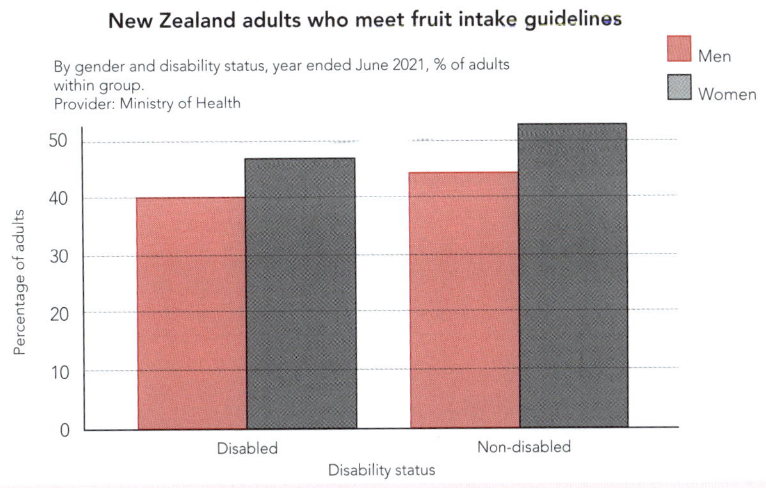

1 A higher percentage of New Zealand women meet fruit intake guidelines than New Zealand men.

☑ Agree ☐ Disagree ☐ Can't tell for sure

Explain your answer. Both disabled and non-disabled women have a higher percentage than their male counterparts.

2 There are more disabled women who meet fruit intake guidelines than non–disabled men.

☐ Agree 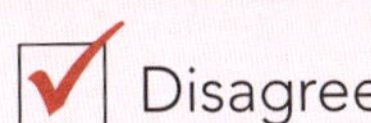 ☑ Disagree ☐ Can't tell for sure

Explain your answer. A higher percentage of disabled women meet the fruit intake guidelines than non-disabled men, not necessarily a higher number.

or 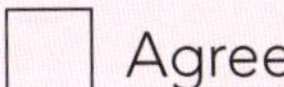 ☐ Agree ☐ Disagree 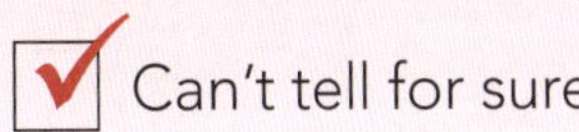 ☑ Can't tell for sure

Explain your answer. A higher percentage of disabled women meet the fruit intake guidelines than non-disabled men, not necessarily a higher number. It is likely that there are fewer disabled women in New Zealand.

Observation: The graph makes it look as though there is a similar number of disabled people and non-disabled people in New Zealand. This is obviously not the case.

ISBN: 9780170447294

1 These are the ACC claims for field hockey injuries in 2021.

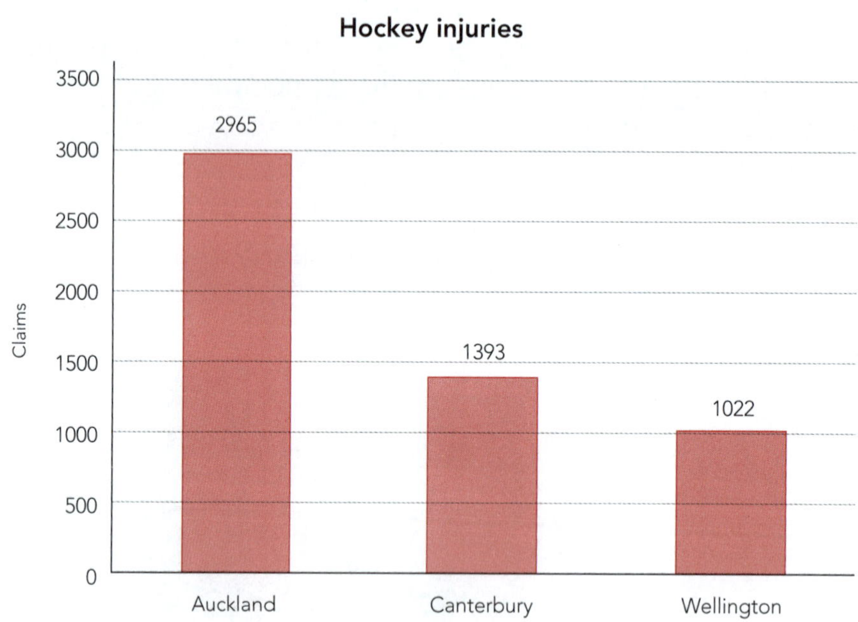

a In 2021 there were more hockey injuries in Auckland than in Canterbury and Wellington combined.

☐ Agree ☐ Disagree ☐ Can't tell for sure

Explain your answer. ______________________________

____

b It's safer to play hockey in Canterbury and Wellington than it is in Auckland.

☐ Agree ☐ Disagree ☐ Can't tell for sure

Explain your answer. ______________________________

____

c This is a fair way of showing this data.

☐ Agree ☐ Disagree

Explain your answer. ______________________________

____

 ISBN: 9780170447294

2 This display shows the qualifications of 15 year olds who left school during 2020. The percentages have been rounded to the nearest whole number.

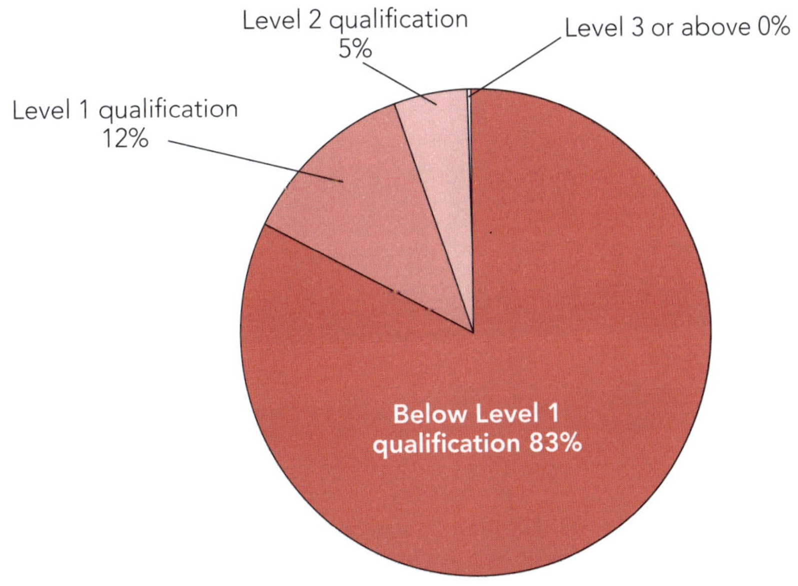

a Very few 15 year olds left school with a Level 1 or higher qualification.

☐ Agree ☐ Disagree ☐ Can't tell for sure

Explain your answer. ______________________________

____

b Fifteen year olds who left school were more than twice as likely to have a Level 1 qualification as a Level 2 qualification.

☐ Agree ☐ Disagree ☐ Can't tell for sure

Explain your answer. ______________________________

____

c No 15 year olds left with a Level 3 or above qualification.

☐ Agree ☐ Disagree ☐ Can't tell for sure

Explain your answer. ______________________________

____

3 This shows the vehicles most commonly stolen in New Zealand 2019–21.

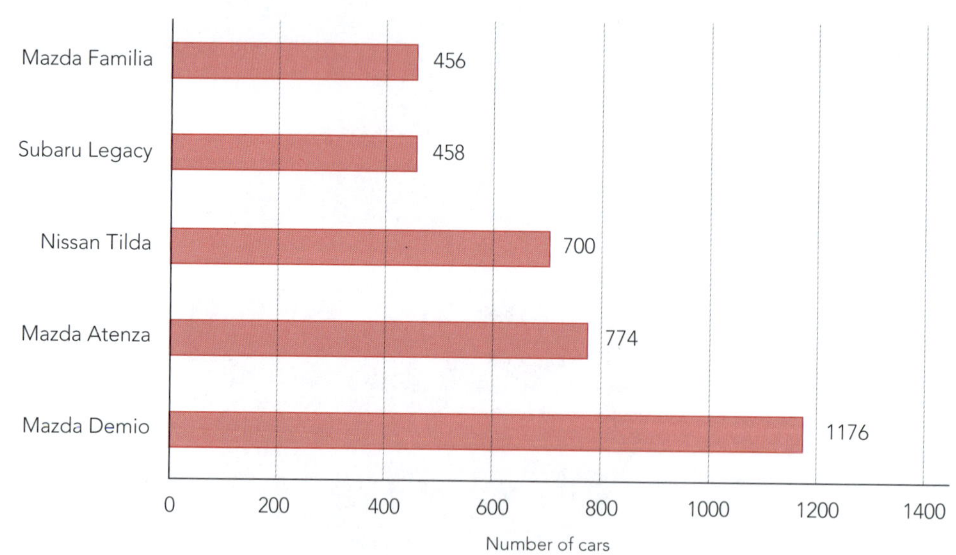

a A Mazda Demio is twice as likely to be stolen as a Subaru Legacy.

☐ Agree ☐ Disagree ☐ Can't tell for sure

Explain your answer. ______________________________

____

b It's not sensible to purchase a Mazda because it is likely to be stolen.

☐ Agree ☐ Disagree ☐ Can't tell for sure

Explain your answer. ______________________________

____

c This is a fair way of showing this data.

☐ Agree ☐ Disagree

Explain your answer. ______________________________

____

 ISBN: 9780170447294

4 Some information about cats in New Zealand.

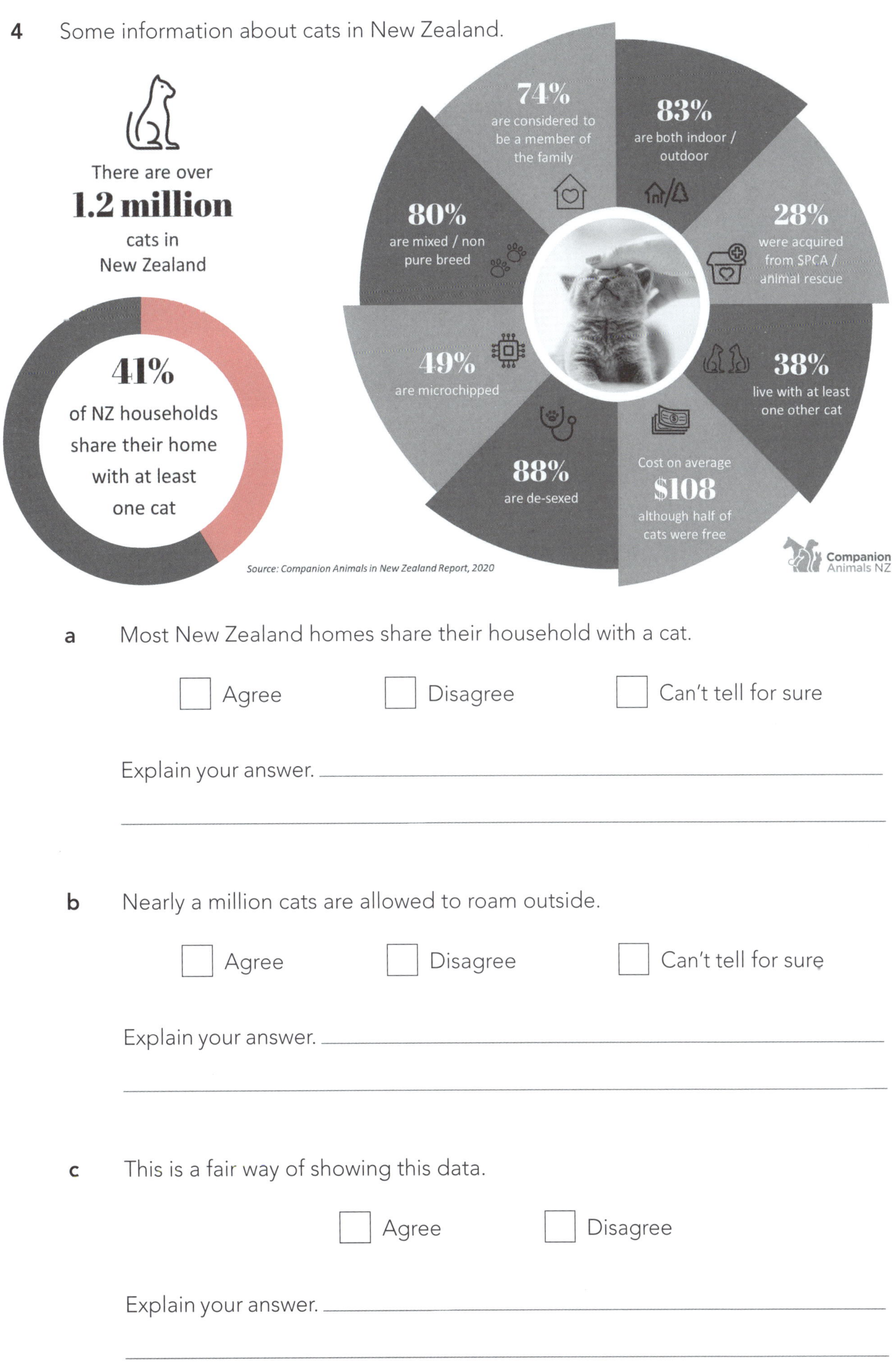

Source: Companion Animals in New Zealand Report, 2020

a Most New Zealand homes share their household with a cat.

☐ Agree ☐ Disagree ☐ Can't tell for sure

Explain your answer. ______________________________

____

b Nearly a million cats are allowed to roam outside.

☐ Agree ☐ Disagree ☐ Can't tell for sure

Explain your answer. ______________________________

____

c This is a fair way of showing this data.

☐ Agree ☐ Disagree

Explain your answer. ______________________________

____

ISBN: 9780170447294

5 The graph shows the number of children who eat fast food at least once a week.

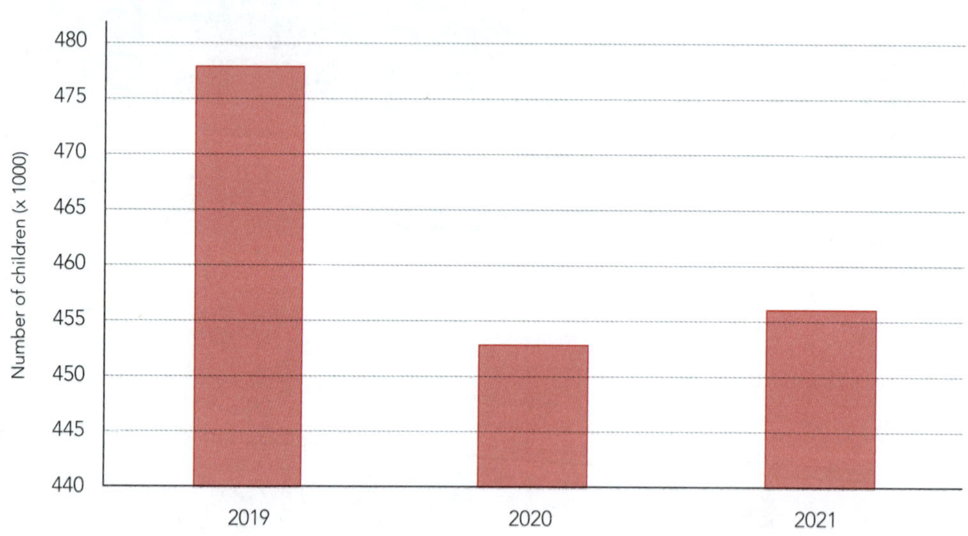

a More than twice as many children ate fast food in 2019 compared with 2021.

☐ Agree ☐ Disagree ☐ Can't tell for sure

Explain your answer. ______________________________

____

b The number of children who ate fast food at least once a week in 2020 was about 453.

☐ Agree ☐ Disagree ☐ Can't tell for sure

Explain your answer. ______________________________

____

c This is a fair way of showing this data.

☐ Agree ☐ Disagree

Explain your answer. ______________________________

____

ISBN: 9780170447294

Revision 1

1 Convert these probabilities into decimals and state which is more likely.

1 in 3 = ________ $\frac{3}{8}$ = ________ More likely: ________

2 At the school fair, it costs $2 to have one spin of this spinner.

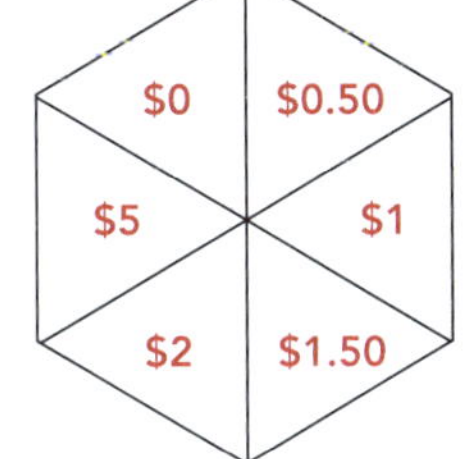

a List the outcomes from one spin (the sample space).

____

b Write the number of outcomes in the sample space.

____

c Calculate the probability of getting nothing back. P = ________

d Calculate the probability of getting at least your money back. P = ________

e Calculate the probability of getting less than $2 back. P = ________

3 a The three types of variables are discrete, descriptive and ____________.

b Give an example of a discrete variable. ____________________

c The distance from your front door to your letterbox is a ____________________ variable.

4 Thirty-four students were asked to select a club to join.

Chess	Photography	Drama	Cooking	No club
8	11	5	2	

Calculate these probabilities if you were to select a student at random.

a P(Photography) ____________________

b P(Drama or Chess) ____________________

c What percentage did not sign up to any of the clubs? ____________________

5 The probability of being born with webbed fingers or toes is around 1 out of 2500. There were 58 659 births in New Zealand in 2021. How many of these babies would you expect to have this condition?

____

ISBN: 9780170447294

6 Eating breakfast and not eating breakfast are examples of ____________________ events.

7 What is the favourite movie of each class member?

This is an example of a ____________________ question.

8 What type of data should be used in a histogram? ____________________

9 Who should be the student representative on the school Board of Trustees?

To find the answer, the school should: ☐ do a census ☐ take a sample

10 Dogs are supposed to be registered every year. Below are the registrations of three dog breeds in New Zealand between 2013 and 2021.

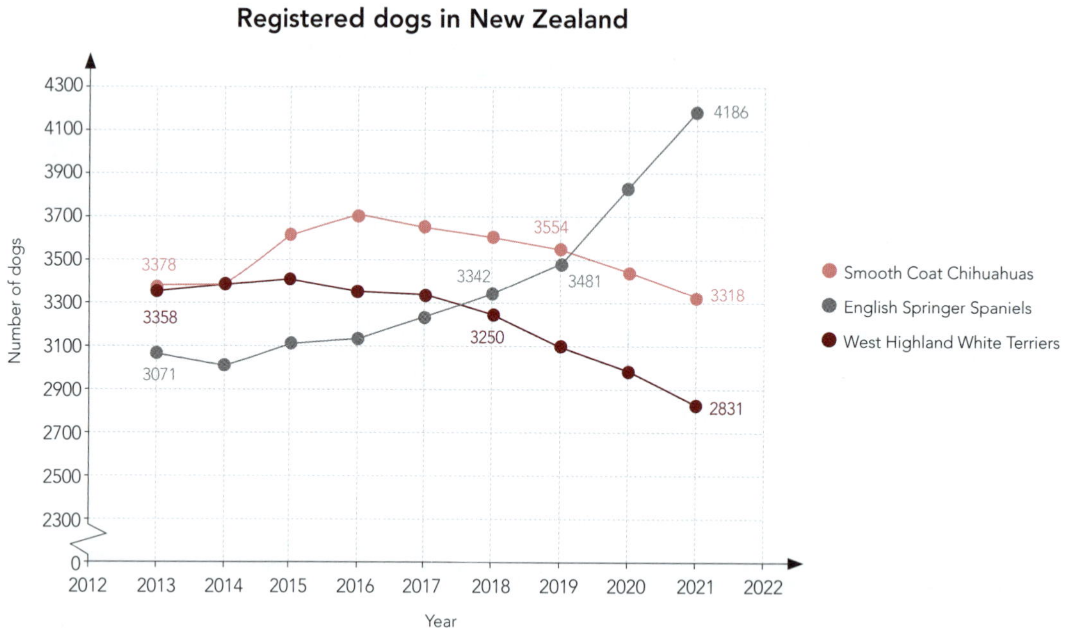

Registered dogs in New Zealand

Number of dogs
4300
4100
3900
3700
3500
3300
3100
2900
2700
2500
2300
0
2012 2013 2014 2015 2016 2017 2018 2019 2020 2021 2022
Year
3378
3358
3071
3342
3250
3554
3481
4186
3318
2831
Smooth Coat Chihuahuas
English Springer Spaniels
West Highland White Terriers

a Which breed has the most registrations in 2013? ____________________

b How many West Highland White Terriers were registered in 2018? __________

c Which breed has had an increase in registrations since 2018? __________

d 'There are more English Springer Spaniels than Smooth Coat Chihuahuas in New Zealand.'

☐ Agree ☐ Disagree ☐ Can't tell for sure

Explain your answer.

____

____

ISBN: 9780170447294

11 **a** The direction of this scatter graph is:

positive/negative

b The strength of this scatter graph is:

strong/moderate/weak

c What are the coordinates of point **f**?

____

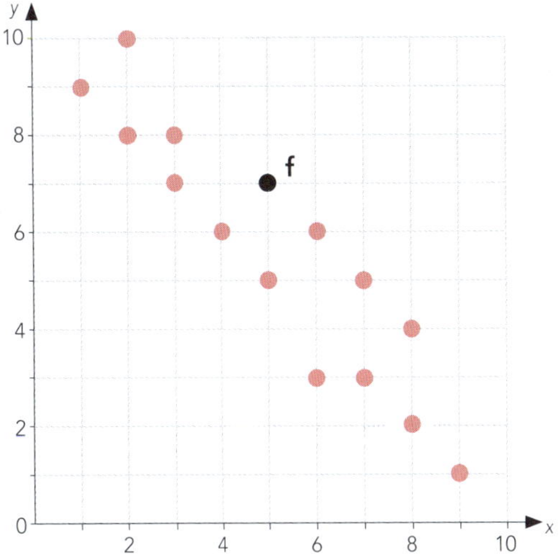

12 Calculate the mean, median, mode and range for this data set:

7 9 10 11 12 15 17 18 19 21 22 24 28

LQ = ______________ Median = ______________ UQ = ______________

Range = ______________ Interquartile range = ______________

13 Fill in the missing percentages and label of this box plot.

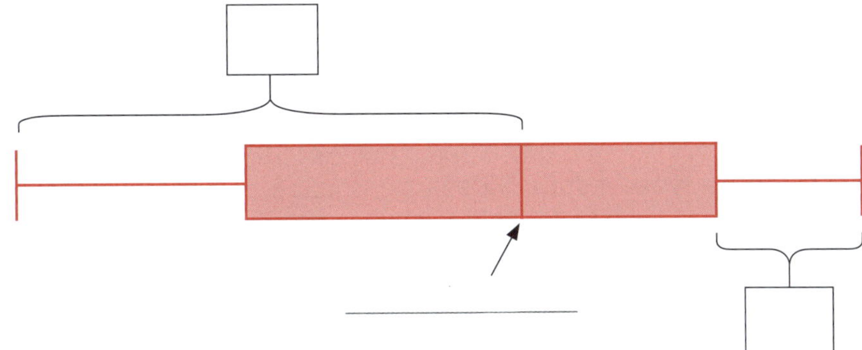

14 The graph shows the number of schools in New Zealand that teach Pacific languages.

a How many schools teach the second most popular Pacific language?

____

b There are approximately 2536 schools in New Zealand. What percentage of them teach Tongan?

____

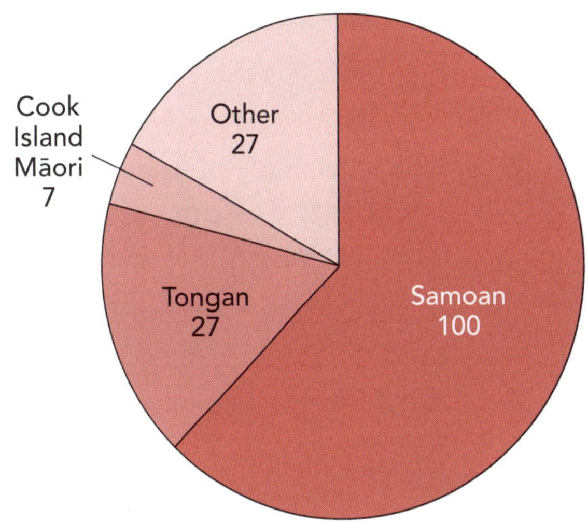

ISBN: 9780170447294

Revision 2

1 Convert these probabilities into decimals and state which is more likely.

1 in 7 = ________ $\frac{3}{20}$ = ________ More likely: ________

2 Students were asked where they would like to go on a school trip.

	Museum	**Art gallery**	**Marae**	**Totals**
Year 9		7	9	
Year 10	12		15	35
Totals	**26**			**65**

a Complete the table.

b What is the probability that a student wanted to go to the marae? ________

c What is the probability that a Year 10 student wanted to go to the art gallery?

____

d What percentage of students are Year 9? ________________

3 **a** The three types of variables are continuous, descriptive and ________.

b Give an example of a continuous variable. ________________

c Your favourite type of chocolate is a ________________ variable.

4 Actual probability is almost always known/unknown.

5 A marble is randomly pulled out of this bag.

a List the outcomes (sample space). ________________

b What is the probability that it is red? P(red) = ________

6 The probability of being born without the ability to smell (anosmia) is approximately 1 in 10 000. The population of the South Island is approximately 1.1 million people. How many people in the South Island would you expect to have this condition?

____

7 Are basketballers taller than rugby players?

This is an example of a ________ question.

 ISBN: 9780170447294

8 What type of data should be used in a scatter graph? ______________________

9 Should New Zealand students have to wear a tie every day to school?

To find the answer, NZ should: ☐ do a census ☐ take a sample

10 ACC collects information on claims made in team sports from 2019 to 2021.

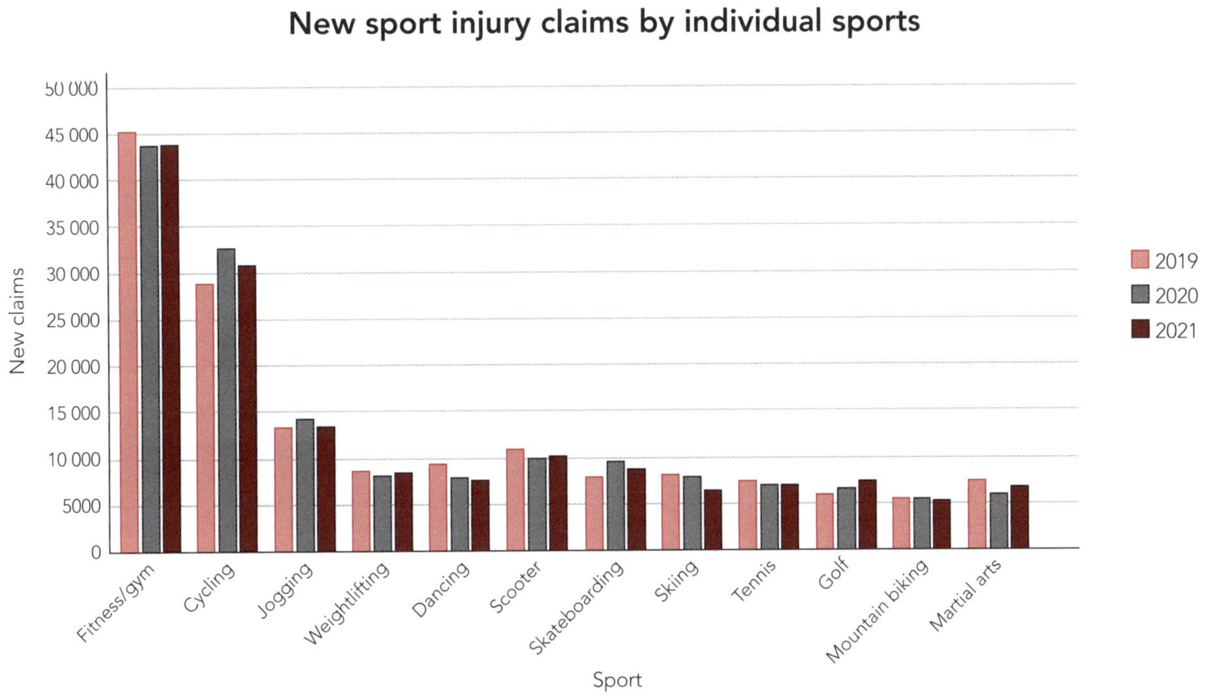

New sport injury claims by individual sports

a In which year were the fewest claims made in skateboarding? ______________________

b Which sport/activity had the most claims in 2021? ______________________

c Which sport/activity has seen an increase in claims each year? ______________________

d Which sport/activity had the biggest increase in claims from 2019 to 2020?

____

e 'It's safer to participate in martial arts than it is to go to the gym in New Zealand.'

☐ Agree ☐ Disagree ☐ Can't tell for sure

Explain your answer. ______________________

____

ISBN: 9780170447294

11 Calculate the mean, median, mode and range for this data set and draw a box plot below.

3 5 7 9 12 12 14 15 15 16 17 18

LQ = ______________ Median = ______________ UQ = ______________

Range = ______________ Interquartile range = ______________

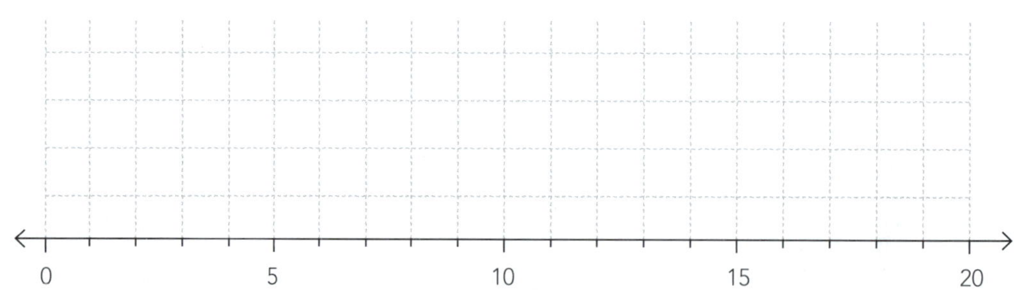

12 This infographic has been made using data from the 2018 census. It describes the population as if New Zealand had 80 adults (over 15 years old).
These are the occupations of the 52 who are employed:

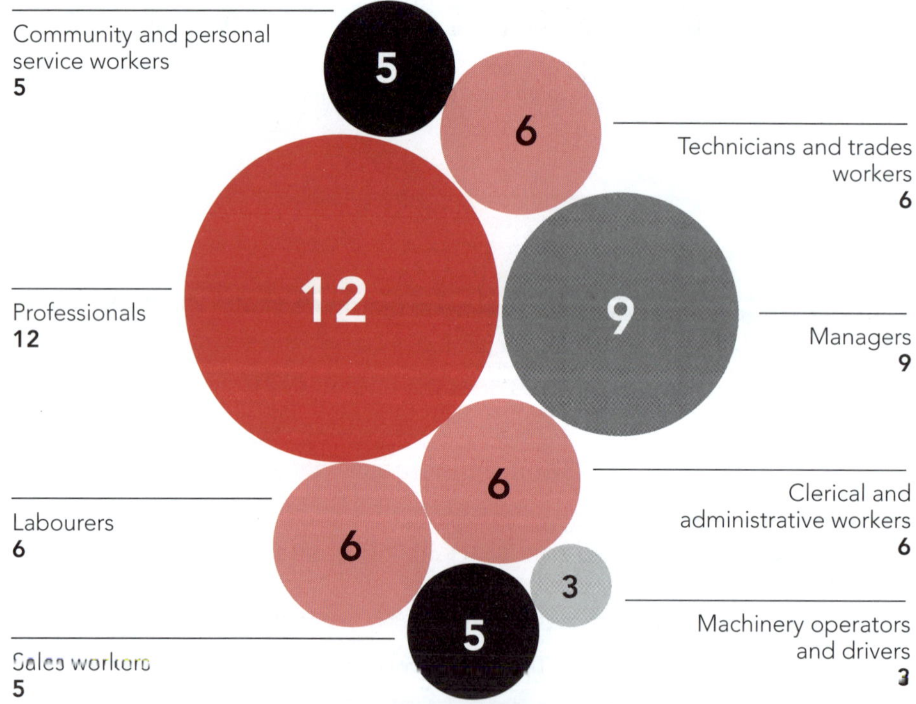

a What percentage of adults were 'professionals'? ______________

b What percentage of those who were employed were sales workers? ______________

c New Zealand had an adult population of around 3.9 million in 2018.
How many of them would you expect to be managers? ______________

ISBN: 9780170447294

Answers

Probability (pp. 6–24)

Fraction, decimal and percentage revision (p. 6)

Shaded circle picture	Fraction	Decimal	Percentage
	$\frac{18}{24} = \frac{3}{4}$	0.75	75%
	$\frac{3}{5}$	0.6	60%
	$\frac{2}{6} = \frac{1}{3}$	$0.\dot{3}$	$33.\dot{3}\%$
	$\frac{3}{8}$	0.75	37.5%
	$\frac{1}{6}$	$0.1\dot{6}$	$16.\dot{6}\%$
	$\frac{26}{39} = \frac{2}{3}$	$0.\dot{6}$	$66.\dot{6}\%$
	$\frac{18}{24} = \frac{7}{8}$	0.875	87.5%

The probability scale (pp. 7–8)

1 You may think of different terms. If so, discuss them with your neighbours or your teacher.

- **1** certain, a sure thing, definite, guaranteed, unquestionable
- **0.9** **very likely**, probable, to be expected
- **0.7** likely, good chance
- **0.5** fifty-fifty, equally likely, maybe
- **0.3** unlikely, probably won't happen
- **0.1** very unlikely, improbable, ghost of a chance, slight chance
- **0** **impossible**, no chance, no way

2 **a** unlikely **b** very likely
c 50:50 chance **d** impossible
e very likely **f** likely
g certain

Using numbers to describe probabilities (p. 9)

1 35% = 0.35 1 in 3 = $0.\dot{3}$

More likely: 35%

2 $\frac{5}{6} = 0.8\dot{3}$ 80:20 = 0.8

More likely: $\frac{5}{6}$

3 65% = 0.65 $\frac{5}{8} = 0.625$

More likely: 65%

4 $\frac{2}{7} = 0.2857$ 1 in 5 = 0.2

More likely: $\frac{2}{7}$

5 P (triplets) = 0.00012 (2 dp), so identical twins are more likely.

6 P(throwing a die four times and getting four 6s) = 0.00077 (2 dp), so tossing a coin 10 times and getting ten heads is more likely.

7 0.000 000 026 (2 sf)

Sample space (pp. 10–12)

1 **a**

Coin	Spinner
H	A
	B
	C
T	A
	B
	C

Outcomes in sample space: HA, HB, HC, TA, TB, TC

Number of outcomes: 6

b

	A	B	C
H	HA	HB	HC
T	TA	TB	TC

Same result: ✓

c Number of outcomes for the coin = 2
Number of outcomes for the spinner = 3
Multiplying these numbers gives 6
Same result? ✓

2 a

Food	Activity	Outcomes
Pizza	Movies	Pizza and movies
	Bowling	Pizza and bowling
Burger	Movies	Burger and movies
	Bowling	Burger and bowling
Sushi	Movies	Sushi and movies
	Bowling	Sushi and bowling

b Number of outcomes: 6

c

	Movies	Bowling
Pizza	Pizza and movies	Pizza and bowling
Burger	Burger and movies	Burger and bowling
Sushi	Sushi and movies	Sushi and bowling

Same result: ✓

d number of food x number of activities = 3 x 2
= 6

Same result? ✓

3 a

Spinner	Coin	Outcome	Probability
R	H	RH	$P(RH) = \frac{1}{6}$
	T	RT	$P(RT) = \frac{1}{6}$
B	H	BH	$P(BH) = \frac{1}{6}$
	T	BT	$P(BT) = \frac{1}{6}$
W	H	WH	$P(WH) = \frac{1}{6}$
	T	WT	$P(WT) = \frac{1}{6}$

b 6

c i $\frac{1}{6}$ or $0.1\dot{6}$ ii $\frac{2}{6}$ or $\frac{1}{3}$ or $0.\dot{3}$

iii $\frac{3}{6}$ or $\frac{1}{2}$ or 0.5 iv $\frac{2}{6}$ or $\frac{1}{3}$ or $0.\dot{3}$

v $\frac{2}{6}$ or $\frac{1}{3}$ or 0.3 vi 0

Ways of calculating probabilities (p. 13)

1 Theoretical 2 Experimental
3 Experimental 4 Theoretical
5 Theoretical

Calculating theoretical probability (pp. 14–16)

1 a \$0, \$5, \$10, \$15, \$20 **b** 5

c $\frac{1}{5}$ or 0.2 d $\frac{4}{5}$ or 0.8

e $\frac{3}{5}$ or 0.6 f 0

2 a

	1	2	3	4	5	6
R	R1	R2	R3	R4	R5	R6
B	B1	B2	B3	B4	B5	B6
W	W1	W2	W3	W4	W5	W6

b 18

c i $\frac{1}{18}$ or $0.0\dot{5}$ ii $\frac{2}{18}$ or $0.\dot{1}$

iii $\frac{9}{18}$ or $0.\dot{5}$ iv $\frac{3}{18}$ or $0.1\dot{6}$

v 0

Challenge 1 (p. 17)

1 a $\frac{3}{9}$ or $\frac{1}{3}$ or $0.\dot{3}$ **b** $\frac{2}{8}$ or $\frac{1}{4}$ or 0.25

c $\frac{3}{8}$ or 0.375 d $\frac{6}{8}$ or 0.75

e $\frac{1}{7}$ or 0.1429 f $\frac{3}{7}$ or 0.4284

g $\frac{6}{7}$ or 0.857

2 a $\frac{5}{16}$ or 0.3125 **b** $\frac{4}{15}$ or $0.2\dot{6}$

c 2 mints, 4 fruit bursts and 8 milkshakes.

d $\frac{4}{14}$ or $\frac{2}{7}$ or 0.26857 e $\frac{6}{14}$ or $\frac{4}{7}$ or 0.5714

Calculating probabilities from observations (pp. 18–20)

1 a 9 **b** $\frac{4}{9}$ or $0.\dot{4}$

c $\frac{5}{9}$ or $0.\dot{5}$

2 a $\frac{21}{28}$ or $\frac{3}{4}$ or 0.75 **b** $\frac{7}{28}$ or $\frac{1}{4}$ or 0.25

3 a 26 **b** $\frac{11}{26}$ or 0.4231

c $\frac{21}{26}$ or 0.8077 d $\frac{10}{26}$ or 0.3846

 ISBN: 9780170447294

4 **a** $\frac{34}{150}$ or $0.22\dot{6}$ **b** $\frac{76}{150}$ or $0.50\dot{6}$

5 **a**

	Experienced	First time	Totals
Sailing	9	45	**54**
Surfing	14	52	**66**
Totals	**23**	**97**	**120**

b $\frac{54}{120}$ or 0.45 **c** $\frac{23}{120}$ or $0.191\dot{6}$

d $\frac{14}{120}$ or $0.11\dot{6}$

e Sailing had $\frac{9}{54}$ or $16.\dot{6}$% experienced.

Surfing had $\frac{14}{66}$ or $21.\dot{2}\dot{1}$% experienced.

So surfing had the greater proportion of experienced students.

6 **a**

	French	Te Reo Māori	Japanese	Totals
Year 9	34	58	25	**117**
Year 10	19	43	21	**83**
Totals	**53**	**101**	**46**	**200**

b $\frac{46}{200}$ or 0.23 **c** $\frac{117}{200}$ or 0.585

d $\frac{58}{200}$ or 0.29 **e** $\frac{21}{83}$ or 0.2530

f $\frac{64}{83}$ or 0.7711

Experimental probability (pp. 21–22)

1 **a**

Die roll	Total	Probability	
1	1	$\frac{1}{10}$	0.1
2	3	$\frac{3}{10}$	**0.3**
3	**3**	$\frac{3}{10}$	**0.3**
4	**1**	$\frac{1}{10}$	**0.1**
5	**0**	$\frac{0}{10}$	**0**
6	**2**	$\frac{2}{10}$	**0.2**

b No. He rolled the die only 10 times. He would need to roll it many more times to prove that 6 is more likely.

c Roll the die many more times.

d

	1	2	3	4	5	6
Frequency	𝍸 𝍸	𝍸 |||	𝍸	𝍸 𝍸		𝍸 ||||	𝍸 ||
Probabilities	$\frac{10}{50}=0.2$	$\frac{8}{50}=0.16$	$\frac{5}{50}=0.1$	$\frac{11}{50}=0.22$	$\frac{9}{50}=0.18$	$\frac{7}{50}=0.14$

e No

Fifty rolls is better, but still not enough to prove the point.

f

	Total	Probability (4 dp)	
6	231	$\frac{231}{1450}$	**0.1593**
Not 6	1219	$\frac{1205}{1450}$	**0.8407**

g No. For the class results, P(6) = 0.1593. If the die is fair, P(6) = $0.1\dot{6}$. The class found that the probability of getting a 6 was slightly lower than the theoretical probability of getting a 6. So the results suggest that George's idea was wrong.

h

Number of tosses	10	50	1450
P(6)	**0.2**	**0.14**	**0.1593**
P(Not 6)	**0.8**	**0.86**	**0.8407**

The probability of getting a 6 gets closer to $0.1\dot{6}$ when the die is rolled more times.

i About 166 667.

j Yes. What you have rolled previously does not affect what you roll next.

Complementary events (p. 23)

1 0.8 **2** 0.37

3 0.24 **4** 0.4138

Expected number (p. 24)

1 45

2 About 142 students (*not* 142.3 — you can't have 0.3 of a student!)

3 12 days

4 200 000

5 72

12

6 **a** 10 168

b About 508 people (*not* 508.4)

Statistical concepts (pp. 25–27)

Census and sample (p. 25)

	Question	Census or sample	Why?
1	A company wants feedback from customers about their new product.	Sample	Too expensive to get feedback from all customers, and while the information matters to the company, is probably not critical.
2	Do New Zealanders still want to belong to the Commonwealth?	Census	Very important issue.
3	What is the most popular car colour in New Zealand?	Sample	Too difficult to collect the colour of every car in New Zealand, and information is not really important.

Types of variables (p. 26)

1 Continuous
2 Discrete
3 Descriptive
4 Continuous
5 C, E
6 A
7 B, D

Investigative questions (p. 27)

1 Summary
2 Relationship
3 Summary
4 Relationship
5 Summary
6 Comparative
7 Comparative
8 Summary
9 Comparative

Data display (pp. 28–51)

1 Dot plot
Discrete
2 **Pie graph**
Descriptive
3 Histogram
Continuous
4 Pictograph
Discrete
5 Tally chart
Discrete and descriptive
6 Box plot
Discrete and continuous
7 Bar graph
Descriptive and discrete
8 Scatter plot
Discrete and continuous
9 Line graph
Discrete and continuous

Pie graphs (pp. 29–30)

1 a 32.5%
b 0.075
c 21

2 a Which bird do you think should be bird of the year?
b Summative
c 14 597
d 39.44%
e 0.1205
f $\frac{3386}{12838} = 0.2637 = 26.37\%$

3 a 0.3523
b 10.81%
c 64.77%
d About 1.8 million or 1 830 000

Reading axes (pp. 31–33)

1 Major: 3
Minor: 1.5

2 Major: 4
Minor: 0.5

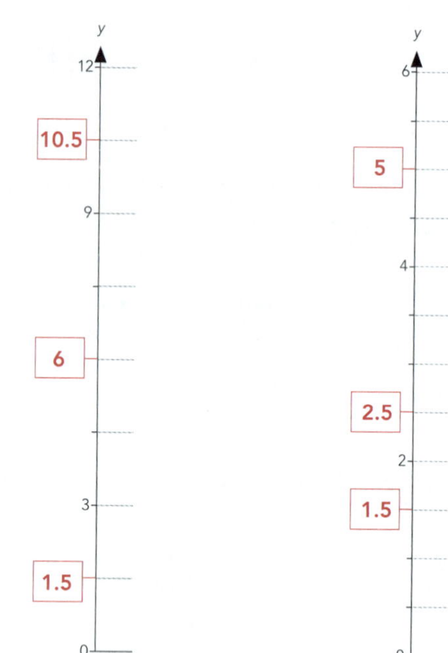

3 Major: 0.2
Minor: 0.1

4 Major: 1
Minor: 0.2

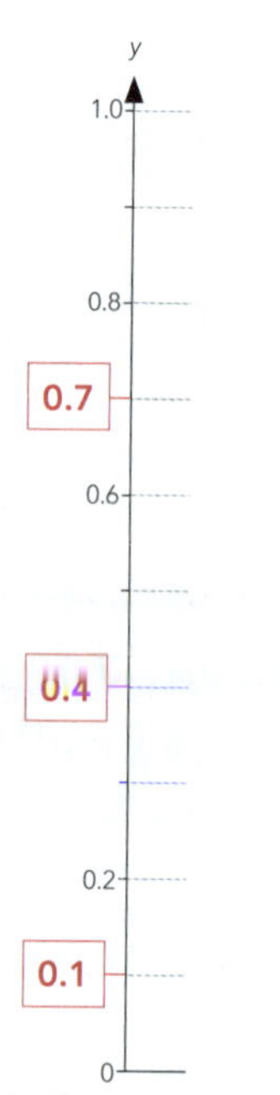

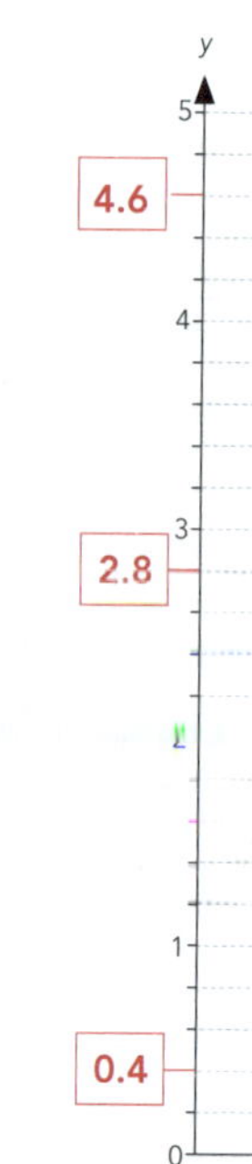

 ISBN: 9780170447294

5 Major: 1 Minor: 0.2

6 Major: 0.5 Minor: 0.05

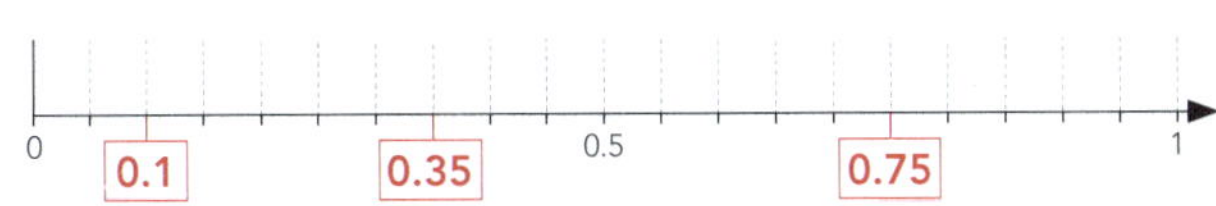

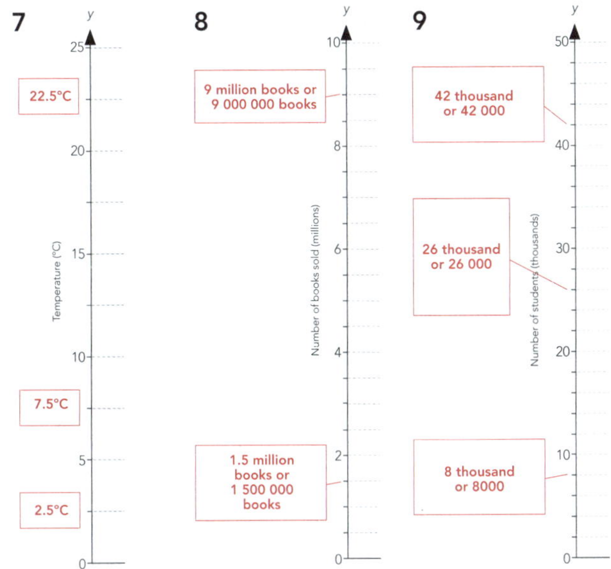

10

11

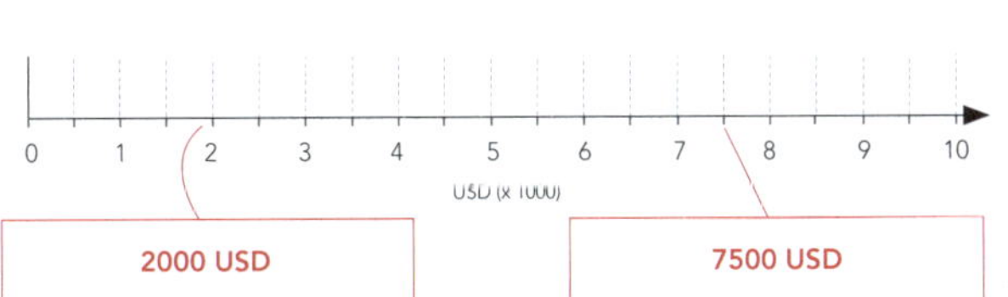

Bar graphs (pp. 34–37)

1 **a** 14 000 birds **b** 25 450

c $\frac{1.9}{25.9 + 0.45 + 1.9 + 14 + 25} \times 100 = 2.8\%$

2 **a** 62% **b** 60.8%

c Disagree. 70.8% of girls brush their teeth at least twice a day, but only 56.9% of boys.

3 **a** White **b** 7 cars

c 18 cars

d Agree. 12 grey cars were electric, but the total for the rest was 11.

4 **a** USA **b** 65

c China **d** Japan

5 **a** What was the difference between the numbers of male and female MPs in each year between 1931 and 2020?

b Comparative **c** 21

d 1969 **e** 120

f 1957: 5%
2020: 48.3%

Line graphs (pp. 38–40)

1 **a** 74.4% **b** 67.6%

c 2012

d 2018 female fruit intake, because there is a decreasing trend for fruit intake for boys and girls from about 2015, but this value showed a sharp increase.

2 **a** 9°C **b** September

c Any value between 2.5 and 2.7°C

d Alexandra

3 **a** How did the prices of avocado, cheese and ham compare over the period between 2012 and 2022?

b Comparative **c** $14

d 2016 **e** 2018

f Avocado

4 **a** Hannah **b** 2010

c Mia

Histograms (pp. 41–42)

1 **a** 60–70 years old **b** 80–90 years old

c 0.1741

2 **a** Summative **b** 6

c 60–80 **d** 12

e $\frac{2}{32}$ or 0.0625

3 **a** 128–130 minutes **b** 7

c 3

Dot plots (pp. 43–46)

1 **a** Summative **b** 9

c 4 **d** $0.208\dot{3}$

e 37.5%

2 **a** 5 **b** 198 cm

c Tall Blacks. The dots for Tall Blacks are mostly further to the right.

d 0.1176

e Agree. There are 17 All Blacks, and only 2 are less than 1.8 m tall and only 2 are more than 2 m tall, so 13 are between 1.8 and 2.0 m.

3 Skewed to the left

4 Bell shaped

5 Irregular

6 Skewed to the right

ISBN: 9780170447294

7 Spread: Distribution **A** is more spread than distribution **B**.
Shape: Distribution A is **skewed to the right**, and distribution B is **bell shaped**.

Scatter plots (pp. 47–51)

1

Artist	Coordinates	Description
a	(**30**, **2.5**)	They used **30** ml of paint and sold it for $**2500**.
b	(**70**, **7**)	They used **70** ml of paint and sold it for $**7000**.

c $500 d 5 ml, $7500
e $0.41\dot{6}$
f

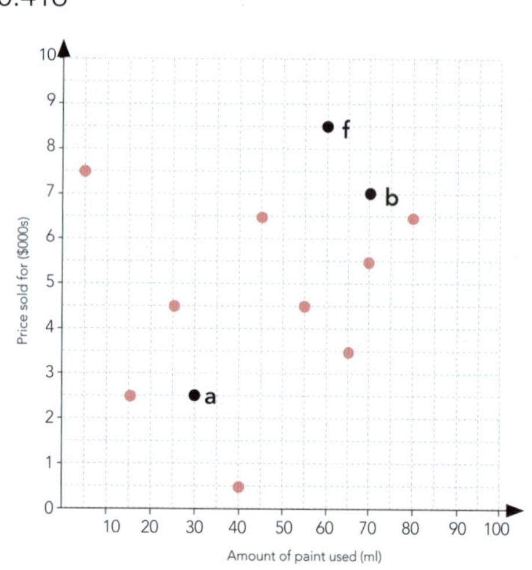

2 a False b True
c True

3

Student	Coordinates	Description
a	(**2.5**, **6**)	They practised for **2.5** hours and made **6** mistakes.
b	(**4.5**, **3**)	They practised for **4.5** hours and made **3** mistakes.

c and **d**

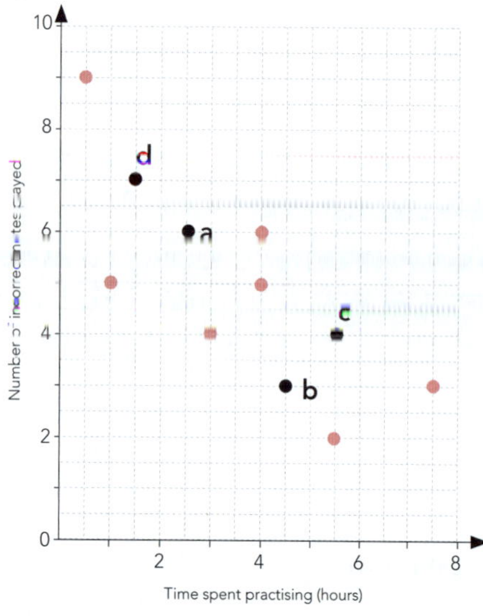

e 45.45%
f In general, students who practised for longer made **fewer** mistakes.

4 **Direction:** Positive
Strength: Strong

5 **Direction:** Negative
Strength: Moderate

6 **Direction:** Positive
Strength: Weak

7 **Direction:** Negative
Strength: Strong

8 The graph shows a **positive** relationship between a person's height and the length of their footprint. This means that taller people have **longer** footprints.

Data analysis (pp. 52–63)

Measures of centre (averages) (pp. 52–55)

1 a 28.83 b 35
c The mean for set **b** is **bigger**/~~smaller~~ than that for set **a** because **the 4 reduced the mean for set a**.

2 a 8.5 b 21.5

3 a 20 b 22

4 a 14 b 17 and 19
c No mode

5 a Mean = 10.75 Median = 10.5
Mode = 10
b Mean = 4.1 Median = 5
Mode = 5
Because it is reduced by the smaller values, especially 0, 1 and 2.
c Mean = 13.5 Median = 13
Mode = 12
Because it includes the two much bigger values (20).

Measures of spread (pp. 56–58)

1 Minimum = 1 LQ = 5 Median = 10
UQ = 15 Maximum = 18
Range = 17 Interquartile range = 10

2 Minimum = 0 LQ = 4 Median = 8.5
UQ = 11 Maximum = 21
Range = 21 Interquartile range = 7

3 Minimum = 2 LQ = 3 Median = 7
UQ = 9 Maximum = 16
Range = 14 Interquartile range = 6

4 Minimum = 7 LQ = 12 Median = 16
UQ = 19.5 Maximum = 24
Range = 17 Interquartile range = 7.5

5 Minimum = 19 LQ = 55 Median = 82.5
UQ = 100 Maximum = 106
Range = 87 Interquartile range = 45

6 Minimum = 1.2 LQ = 1.3 Median = 1.4
UQ = 1.8 Maximum = 1.9
Range = 0.7 Interquartile range = 0.5

 ISBN: 9780170447294

7 Minimum = 1 LQ = 3 Median = 4
UQ = 5 Maximum = 9
Range = 8 Interquartile range = 2

8 Minimum = 21 LQ = 27 Median = 32
UQ = 35.5 Maximum = 40
Range = 19 Interquartile range = 8.5

9 Minimum = 11 LQ = 12 Median = 12
UQ = 14 Maximum = 20
Range = 9 Interquartile range = 2

Unusual features (pp. 59–62)

1

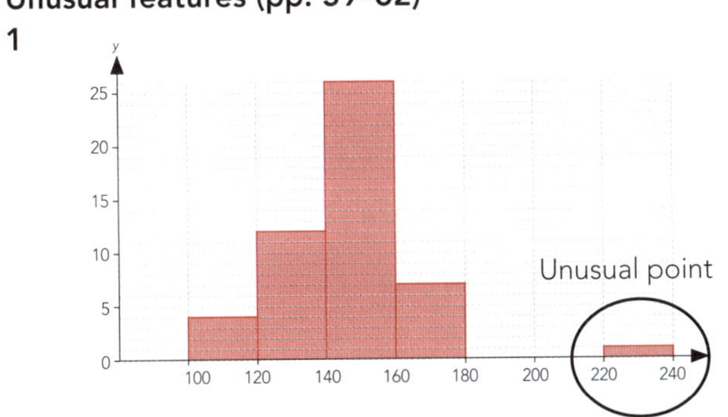

2 Cluster

3 Unusual point

Cluster

4 35 29 25 27 (13) 29 32 51 32 34

Unusual point

5

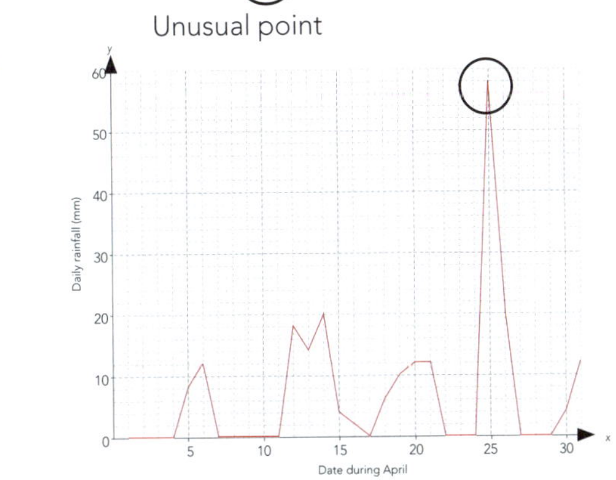

On every other day, the maximum amount of rain was 20 mm. On the 25th, there was 59 mm rain.

6 Median = 8.5 Mean = 11
Best measure(s) of centre: **median**, because **only two values out of nine are above the mean**.

7 Median = 18 Mean = $18.\dot{6}$
Best measure(s) of centre: **either**, because **there's isn't much difference between them**.

8 Median = 73 Mean = 63.6
Best measeue(s) of centre: **median**, because **it's nearer the centre of the data**.

9 Median = 10.5 Mean = 10.318
Best measure(s) of centre: **either**, because **both are close to the centre of the data**.

10 Median = 7 Mean = 5.9375
Best measure(s) of centre: **median**, because **most of the data is 6 or more**.

Challenge 2 (p. 63)

1 a 17 b 7
c 9 d 7
e 9, 10 f 5, 17

2 a 5 b 10
c 8

3

Set A	8	3	6
Set B	7	**4**	**6**
Set C	9	**3**	**5**

Box plots (pp. 64–68)

1

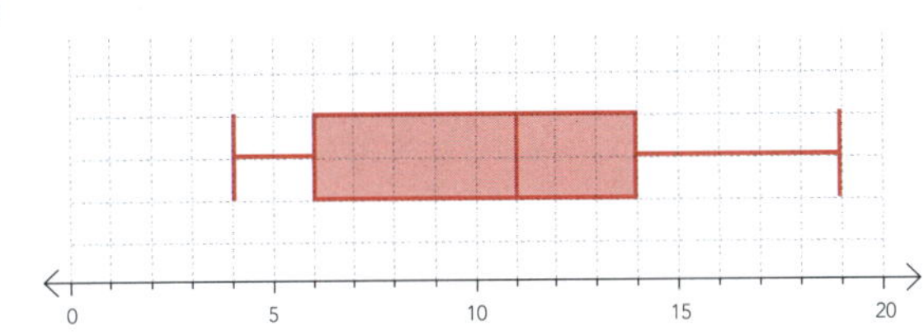

2 Minimum = 2 LQ = 5 Median = 8
UQ = 16 Maximum = 19

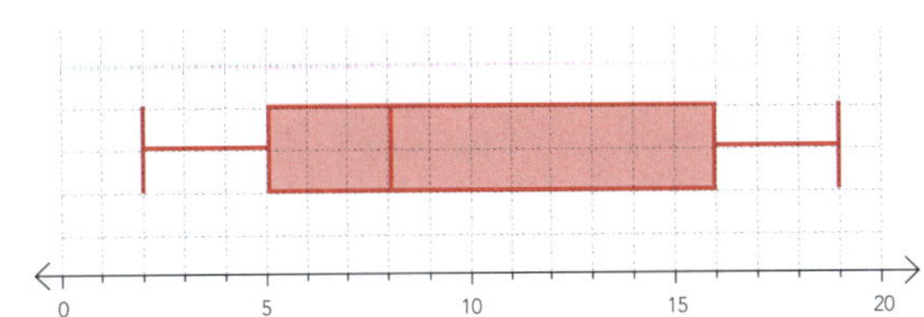

3 Minimum = 0 LQ = 4.5 Median = 10
UQ = 16.5 Maximum = 20

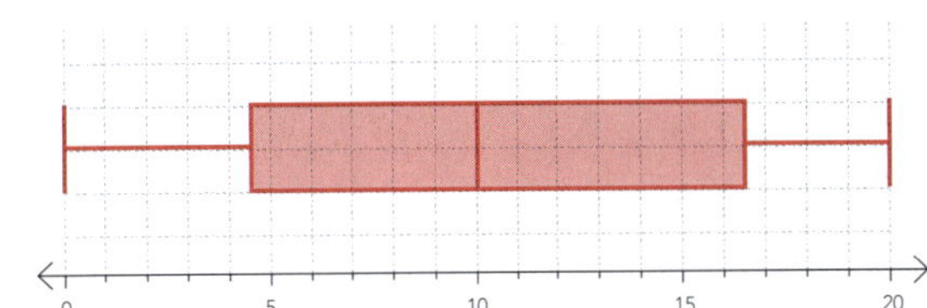

ISBN: 9780170447294

4 Minimum = 0 LQ = 3 Median = 7
UQ = 13 Maximum = 19

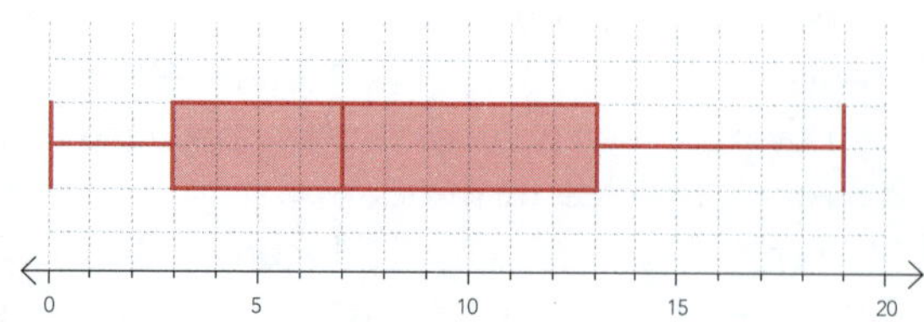

Understanding box plots (pp. 66–67)

1

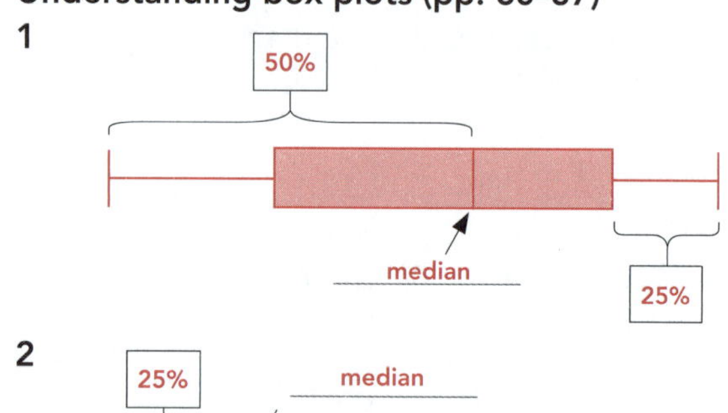

2

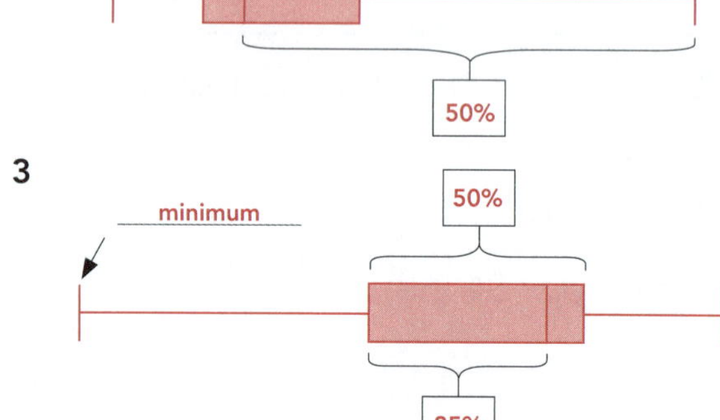

3

minimum

50%

25%

4

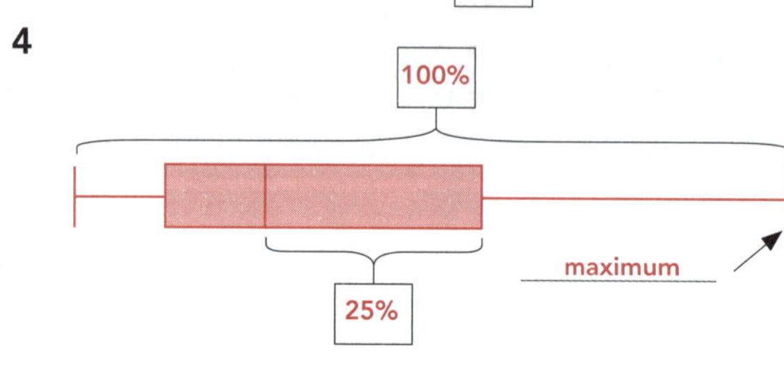

Comparing box plots (p. 68)

1 a ✓ b ✓
c ×
2 a × b ×
c ✓

Infographics (pp. 69–71)

1 a 2086 m
b Round Hill
c 484 m
2 a 27%
b 51.38 billion litres
c US$130.8 billion
3 a TV2
b TV3
c YouTube and TV1
d Some people would have used several of these channels.
4 a TVNZ
b 22%
c TV3
d Stuff
e 33.3%
5 a 7%
b Natural and physical sciences
c Engineering and related technologies
d i 32 780
ii 108 025
iii 51 405

Statistical literacy (pp. 72–80)

Sampling and bias (pp. 74–75)

1

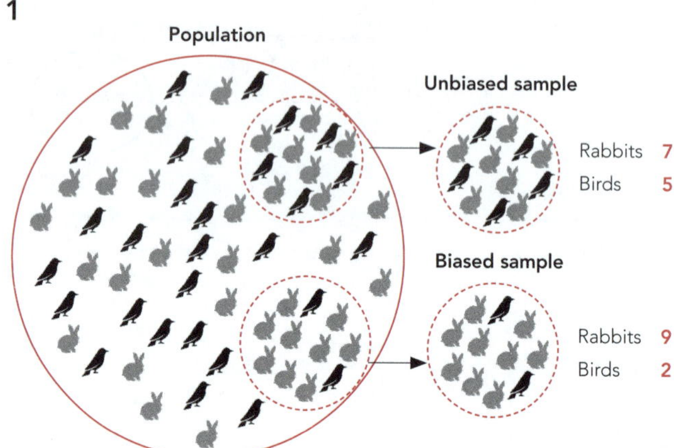

2 Big enough sample? ×
Fair or biased? Biased
Not many students would have surnames beginning with 'Y', and probably no Asian, Māori or Pasifika students.
3 Big enough sample? ×
Fair or biased? Biased
Small group of just girls.
4 Big enough sample? ✓
Fair or biased? Fair
Everybody has to come through the gate, and taking a tenth of the school roll should be a big enough sample.
5 Big enough sample? ✓
Fair or biased? Biased
Those who arrive promptly will probably have different views compared with those who are later.
6 Those who drive through to collect their food may prefer different products compared with those who dine in.
7 People at the bowls club are likely to be older than those who don't go there.

ISBN: 9780170447294

8 Only people with strong views are likely to bother to text or email their views, and some older people may not use texts or email, so they would be excluded.
9 Ute drivers are probably more likely to be male and younger than those who drive other types of vehicles.
10 Members of the garden club will almost certainly have different views regarding trees than the general public.

Question types and appropriate data displays (p. 74)

1 Question type: Comparative
Graph types: Tally chart, Bar graph
2 Question type: Summary
Graph type: Line graph
3 Question type: Summary
Graph type: Bar graph, Pie graph, Tally chart
4 Question type: Relationship
Graph type: Scatter graph
5 Question type: Summary
Graph type: Tally chart, Histogram
6 Question type: Summary
Graph type: Line graph
7 Question type: Comparative
Graph type: Bar graph

Data interpretation (pp. 75–80)

1 **a** Agree
There was a total of 2415 injuries in Canterbury and Wellington, and there were 2965 in Auckland.
b Can't tell for sure
There is no information on how many hockey players there are in each centre. A higher percentage could be injured in Dunedin.
c Either: Agree
If all you want to know is the total number of injuries, this shows the information well.
Or: Disagree
If you want to know the differences between injury rates, then you need to know the numbers of players in each centre.

2 **a** Agree
83% left with below Level 1 qualification.
b Agree
12 % left with a Level 1 qualification and 5% left with al Level 2 qualification.
c Can't tell for sure
If there were only one or two, their percentage may have been rounded down to 0.

3 **a** Either: Agree
Agree as a rough estimate, but it is actually more than two and a half times more likely to be stolen.
Or: Disagree
It is actually more than two and a half times more likely to be stolen.
b Can't tell for sure
We have no information about other Mazda models, nor the numbers of each model that are sold.
c Either: Agree
If all you want to know is the total numbers of cars stolen, this shows the information well.
Or: Disagree
If you want to know the differences between proportions stolen for each model, then you need to know the numbers of each model on the road.

4 **a** Disagree
The infographic states that 41% of homes have at least one cat.
b Agree
83% of cats are both indoor and outdoor and there are over 1.2 million cats in New Zealand. So 996 000 are allowed outside, which is nearly one million.
c Disagree
All the sectors around the 'pie' diagram are the same size but they represent different percentages.

5 **a** Disagree
Because in 2019 about 478 000 ate fast food but in 2021 about 456 000 ate fast food, which is nowhere near half of 478 000.
b Disagree
It was 453 000.
c Disagree
Because the vertical axis starts at 440 000, so the true proportions of the bars are not shown.

Revision 1 (pp. 81–83)

1 1 in 3 = $0.\dot{3}$ $\quad \frac{3}{8} = 0.375$ $\quad$ More likely: $\frac{3}{8}$

2 **a** \$0, \$0.50, \$1, \$1.50, \$2, \$5
b 6
c P(nothing) = $\frac{1}{6}$ or $0.1\dot{6}$
d P(money back) = $\frac{2}{6}$ or $\frac{1}{3}$ or $0.\dot{3}$
e P(less than \$2) = $\frac{4}{6}$ or $\frac{2}{3}$ or $0.\dot{6}$

ISBN: 9780170447294

3 a continuous
  b Shoe size, or anything that has to be counted. (Check with your teacher if you have something different.)
  c continuous

4 a P(Photography) = $\frac{11}{34}$ or 0.32 (2 dp)
  b P(Drama or Chess) = $\frac{13}{26} = \frac{1}{2}$
  c 24% (0 dp)

5 23 or 24 babies (not 23.46 (2 dp))

6 complementary

7 summary

8 Continuous

9 do a census

10 a Smooth Coat Chihuahuas
  b 3250
  c English Springer Spaniels
  d Either: Agree
  Agree assuming all dogs are registered. Even if they are not, the difference is large, so it is unlikely that the statement is false.
  Or: Can't tell for sure
  There are more English Springer Spaniels registered in New Zealand in 2021. However, not all dogs are registered so we can't tell for sure.

11 a negative
  b strong
  c (5, 7)

12 7, 9, 10, 11, 12, 15, 17, 18, 19, 21, 22, 24, 28
  LQ = 10.5 Median = 17
  UQ = 21.5 Range = 21
  Interquartile range = 11

13

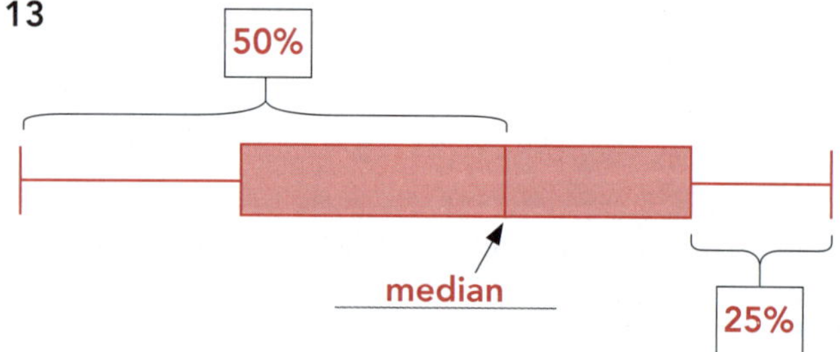

14 a 27
  b 1.06% (2 dp)

Revision 2 (pp. 84–86)

1 1 in 7 = 0.43 (2dp) $\frac{3}{20} = 0.15$ More likely: $\frac{3}{20}$

2 a

	Museum	Art gallery	Marae	Totals
Year 9	14	7	9	**30**
Year 10	12	8	15	**35**
Totals	**26**	**15**	**24**	**65**

  b $\frac{24}{65}$ or 0.369 (3 dp) c $\frac{8}{35}$ or 0.23 (2 dp)
  d 46.15% (2 dp)

3 a discrete
  b Height, weight, distance to school, etc. Anything that has to be measured. (Check with your teacher if you have something different.)
  c descriptive

4 unknown

5 a red, black
  b P(red) = $\frac{3}{7}$ or 0.43 (2 dp)

6 110

7 comparative

8 Continuous or discrete

9 take a sample

10 a 2019
  b Fitness/gym
  c Golf
  d Cycling
  e Can't tell for sure
  It is likely that far more people go to the gym or do fitness than those who participate in martial arts. We do not know how risky each activity is.

11 LQ = 8 Median = 13
  UQ = 15.5 Range = 15
  Interquartile range = 7.5

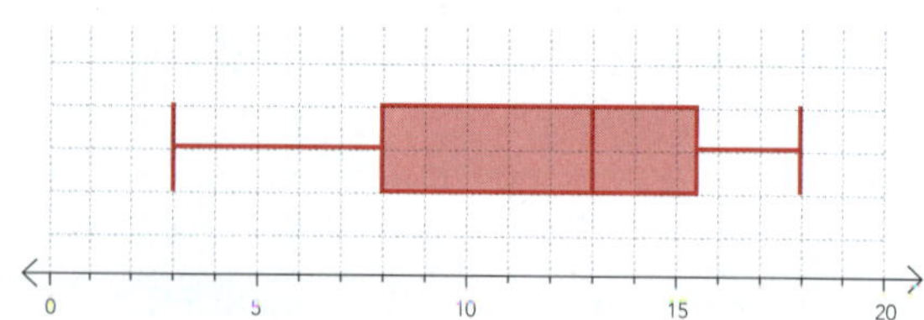

12 a 15%
  b 9.02% (2 dp)
  c About 440 000

 ISBN: 9780170447294